WATERLOO MUSIC PRESENTS

THE
LAWLESS THEORY COURSE

GRADE ONE
THEORY

The material in this book covers the examination requirements
for the Grade 1 Theory Course
of the Royal Conservatory of Music of Toronto
and the Western Ontario Conservatory of Music.

PUBLISHER

WATERLOO
MUSIC

ISBN: 0 - 88909 - 007 - 6

First Printing: 1975	Tenth Printing: 1986
Second Printing: 1976	Eleventh Printing: 1987
Third Printing: 1978	Twelfth Printing: 1988
Fourth Printing: 1979	Thirteenth Printing: 1989
Fifth Printing: 1980	Fourteenth Printing: 1990
Sixth Printing: 1981	Fifteenth Printing: 1991
Seventh Printing: 1983	Sixteenth Printing: 1992
Eighth Printing: 1984	Seventeenth Printing: 1993
Ninth Printing: 1986	Eighteenth Printing: 1994

The Author

James Lawless is a graduate of the Faculty of Music, University of Toronto, and the Royal Conservatory of Music and St. Michaels Choir School in Toronto.

He has been on the staff of the Royal Conservatory of Music since 1964 as a teacher of piano and theoretical subjects and prior to this taught at the Hamilton Conservatory of Music and St. Michaels Choir School in Toronto.

For many years Mr. Lawless was involved with the summer program of the Ontario Society for Crippled Children where he held the positions of musical director and program director.

As a member of the Board of Examiners he has travelled extensively across Canada. He is well known as an adjudicator of music festivals and as a workshop specialist.

He is co-author of the widely received harmony series: *Writing Music — Books One, Two and Three.*

James Lawless is now Chief Examiner for the Royal Conservatory of Music of Toronto.

Preface

After many years of teaching theory of music, Mr. Lawless has given us a thoroughly musical and practical approach to the basics of creating music.

Though primarily for use in the preparation of examinations in the grade one rudiments of music, this book will be of value to any student of music, due to its systematic development and its practical application to the keyboard.

It is with pleasure that I endorse this valuable addition to our music literature.

Clifford McAree
Mus. Bac., L.R.C.T.
F.R.C.C.O. (Hon. Causa)
Royal Conservatory of Music

Foreword

The key to the approach taken in this text is "programmed-learning" — the educationally proven technique that makes it easier for students to progress through the fundamentals of music theory with a far greater degree of comprehension.

Explanations are direct, intentionally simple and easy for students to understand.

Ear training and theory-related keyboard applications are provided as optional lessons throughout the text.

There is an abundant supply of written exercises, summaries, review exercises and tests which are graded, so that students can themselves evaluate their progress. This stimulates greater involvement and provides an incentive to students endeavor to do their best. Another practical service it provides is an indication to teachers of those areas requiring further review.

This "programmed-learning" technique allows students to progress at their own pace and still provides all of the necessary direction and guidance to foster maximum achievement and reward. This should make students more knowledgeable musicians and should result in higher marks on examinations.

It is my sincere desire that teachers have a book that they find educationally sound and useful and that students enjoy learning more about the inner workings of music.

James Lawless

For those of you wishing to ask questions or express your views personally, I would welcome your correspondence at this address:

James Lawless
Chief Examiner,
Royal Conservatory of Music,
Toronto, Ontario, Canada

Sections

Technical Names for the Notes of a Scale 5

Accidentals 8

Major Scales 11

Minor Scales 25

Compound Time 34

Intervals 54

Chords 64

Naming the Keys of Melodies without Key Signatures 75

Transposition 82

Cadences 91

Correction of Errors 98

Level One Test Paper 99

Common Terms and Signs 106

Answers to Written Exercises 111

Appendix 112

*Grateful thanks are offered to Sister Caroline Bering, Joe Caringi, Kelly Holme,
Rita Hunt, Suzanne Langor, and Dr. Lorraine Thibeault
who gave detailed descriptions of errors in the previous editions
which have been corrected herewith.*

Technical Names for the Notes of a Scale

In Book One we learned that a scale is an alphabetical arrangement of eight notes beginning and ending on the same note, e.g., C – C, D – D, etc. Each note is a different "degree" of the scale and can be given its own technical name (regardless of where it is written or played).

1. **Tonic** — is the first "degree" note of any scale.

2. **Supertonic** — is the second "degree" note of any scale.

3. **Mediant** — is the third "degree" note of any scale. It lies midway between the tonic and dominant.

4. **Subdominant** — is the fourth "degree" note of any scale. It is the same note as the fifth (dominant) below (sub) the tonic.

5. **Dominant** — is the fifth "degree" note of any scale.

6. **Submediant** — is the sixth "degree" note of any scale. It is the same note as the third (mediant) below (sub) the Tonic.

7. **Leading Note** — is the seventh "degree" note of any scale.

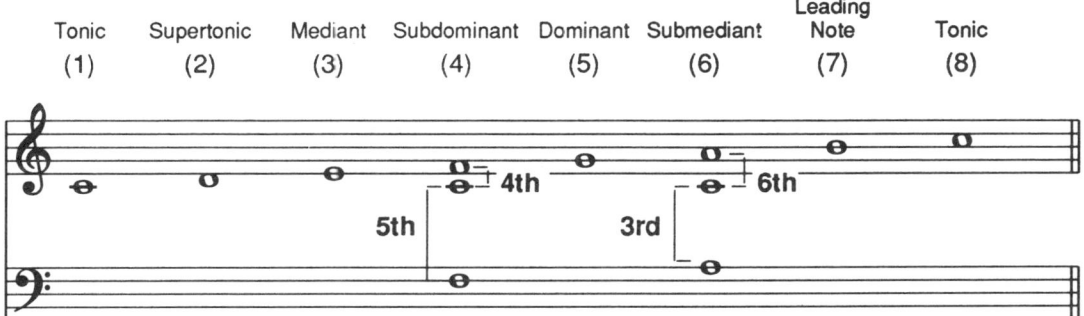

| Tonic (1) | Supertonic (2) | Mediant (3) | Subdominant (4) | Dominant (5) | Submediant (6) | Leading Note (7) | Tonic (8) |

Remember —

The seventh "degree" note of the minor scale is always raised a semitone.

Review Exercise

Write the following notes, adding the correct key signature:

a) the *subdominant* note in the keys of C major, B minor

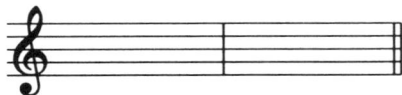

b) the dominant note in the keys of B flat major, F minor

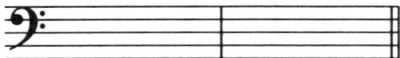

c) the tonic note in the keys of G minor, A major

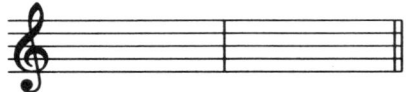

d) the mediant note in the keys of C minor, F sharp minor, E major

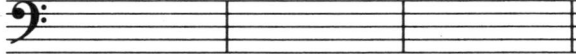

e) the leading note in the keys of G major, C sharp minor, A minor

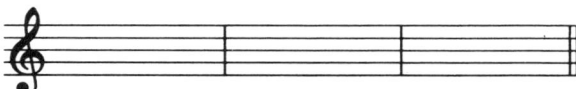

f) the submediant note in the keys of A flat major, D minor, E minor

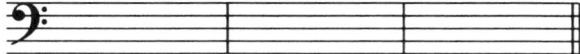

g) the supertonic note in the keys of D major, F major, E flat major

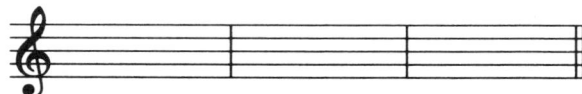

Perfect Score: 18   Student's Score:

Keyboard Exercise (optional)

1. Name the key.

2. Play each of the following notes, saying aloud its technical name in the given key.

Key _____ Major

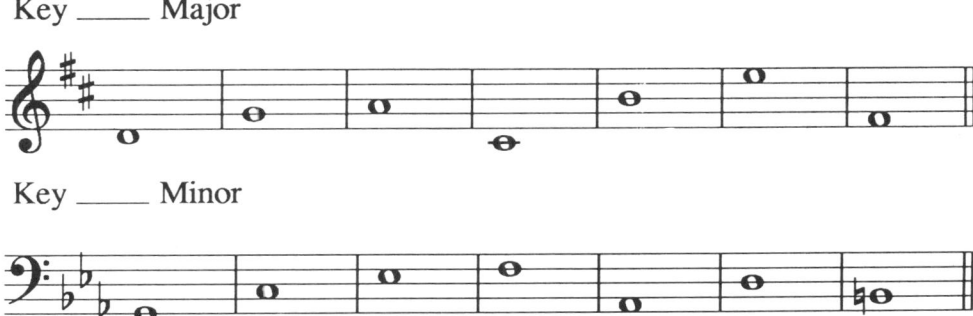

Key _____ Minor

Review

1. Each note is a different_____of the scale and can be given its own name.

2. The second degree note of the scale is called the_____; the fourth degree note is the_____; the seventh degree note is the_____; the fifth degree note is the_____; the first degree note is the_____; and the sixth degree note is the _____.

3. The subdominant note of the scale is the same note as the_____ note below the tonic.

4. The submediant note of the scale is the same note as the_____note below the tonic.

Perfect Score: 12   Student's Score:

Accidentals

An accidental is a sign used by composers to alter a note(s) by means of adding a sharp (♯), flat (♭) or natural (♮). This note is altered only temporarily, and the accidental should never be considered as part of the key signature.

The rules for writing and playing notes with accidentals are:

a) Notes that have sharps, flats or naturals are only altered temporarily.

b) Notes altered by an accidental, sharp, flat or natural remain changed for only one measure, unless tied into the next measure.

c) The altered note remains changed if played a second time within the bar or measure, unless it is altered by another accidental.

Here are two more accidentals:

The Double Sharp

When a composer writes this sign (✗) beside a note, it means that the note is to be played two semitones (a whole tone) higher. The double sharp sign can be written in two ways:

a) beside the note on the staff

e.g.,

Remember that the double sharp is always written on the left side of the note on the same line or space as the note.

b) beside the letter name of the note

e.g., C✗, F✗, A✗

Remember that the double sharp is always written on the right side of the letter name.

Remember: Double sharp notes are played on the white key two semitones (a whole tone) higher, with the exception of E✗ and B✗, which are played on the black key two semitones (a whole tone) higher.

Keyboard Exercise (optional)

a) Find and play each of these notes in several locations (treble and bass) on the keyboard: C, C♯, C⨯, F, F♯, F⨯, A, A♯, A⨯.

b) Find and play: E, E♯, E⨯, and B, B♯, B⨯.

c) *Teacher:* Ask the student to find and play any double sharp note on the keyboard.

Written Exercise (to be completed at the lesson)

a) Re-write the following notes with a double sharp sign.

b) Write the letter name of each double sharp note below the staff.

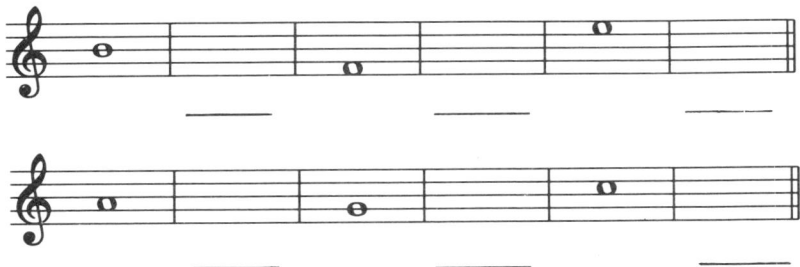

| Perfect Score: 6 | Student's Score: |

The Double Flat

When a composer writes this sign (♭♭) beside a note, it means that the note is to be played two semitones (a whole tone) lower. The double flat sign can be written in two ways:

a) Beside the note on the staff. Remember that the double flat is always written on the left side of the note on the same line or space as the note.

e.g.,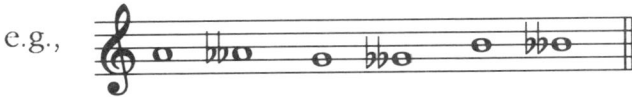

b) Beside the letter name of the note. Remember that the double flat sign is always written on the right side of the letter name,

e.g., A♭♭, G♭♭, B♭♭

Remember: Double flat notes are played on the white key two semitones (a whole tone) lower, with the exception of F♭♭ and C♭♭, which are played on the black key two semitones (a whole tone) lower.

Review

1. **Name five accidentals used by composers to alter temporarily the pitch of notes:** _____ _____ _____ _____ _____

2. **The double sharp is always written on the_____side of the note on the staff and on the_____side of the letter name.**

3. **The double sharp means that the note is to be played_____ _____ (a whole tone) higher.**

4. **The double flat is always written on the_____side of the note on the staff and on the_____side of the letter name.**

5. **The double flat means that the note is to be played____ _____ (a whole tone) lower.**

Perfect Score: 13   Student's Score:

Keyboard Exercise (optional)

a) Find and play each of these notes in several locations (treble and bass) on the keyboard: D, D♭, D♭♭, G, G♭, G♭♭, B, B♭, B♭♭.

b) Find and play: F, F♭, F♭♭, C, C♭, C♭♭.

c) *Teacher:* Ask the student to find and play any double flat note on the keyboard.

Written Exercise (to be completed at the lesson)

a) Re-write the following notes with a double flat sign.
b) Write the letter name of each double flat.

Perfect Score: 6
Student's Score:

Major Scales

Written and Keyboard (optional) Exercise

(It is recommended that these be done at the keyboard where the student can see the notes and listen to the sounds.)

a) Name the key of the following major scales (1 mark).

b) Mark the tone ⊓ and semitone ⊓ intervals in the following scales, adding accidentals (sharps) where necessary (7 marks). The order of tones and semitones in the major scale is: T, T, S, T, T, T, S.

Scale of _____ Major

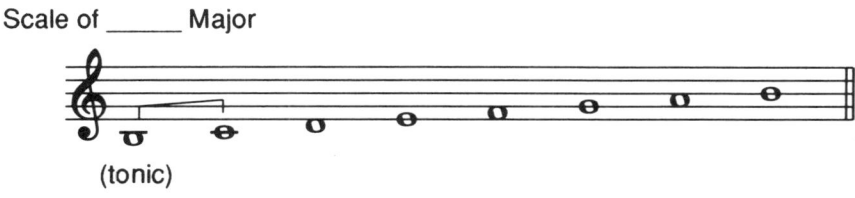

(tonic)

Scale of _____ Major

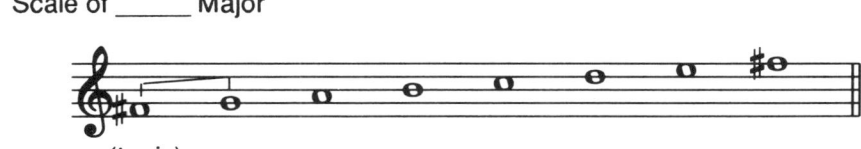

(tonic)

Scale of _____ Major

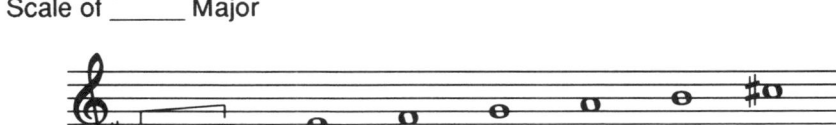

(tonic)

Perfect Score: 24   Student's Score:

Keyboard Exercise (optional)

Play each of these major scales: C, G, D, A, E, B, F♯, C♯.

Written and Keyboard (optional) Exercise

(It is recommended that these be done at the keyboard where the student can see the notes and listen to the sounds.)

a) Name the key of the following major scales (1 mark).

b) Mark the tone ⊓ and semitone ⊓ intervals in the following scales, adding accidentals (sharps) where necessary (7 marks).

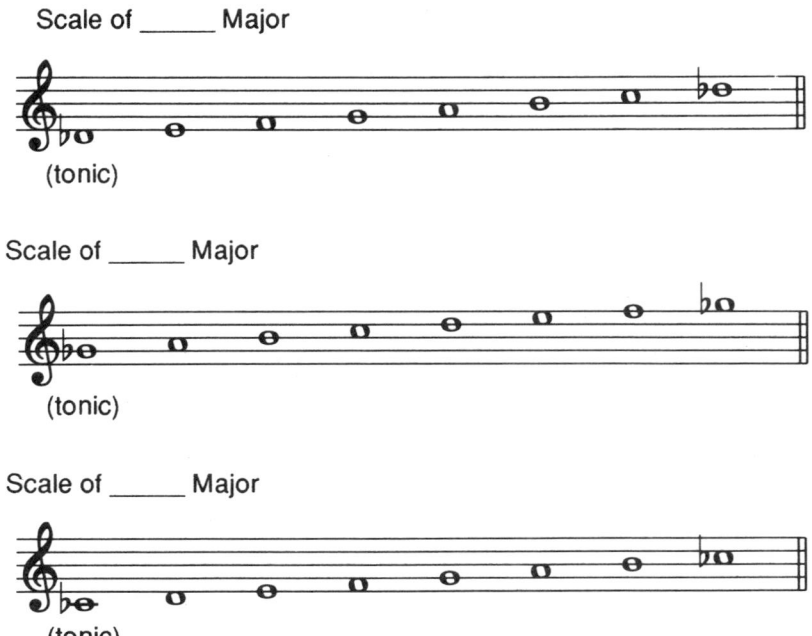

Scale of _____ Major

(tonic)

Scale of _____ Major

(tonic)

Scale of _____ Major

(tonic)

Perfect Score: 24   Student's Score:

Keyboard Exercise (optional)

Play each of these major scales: F, B flat, E flat, A flat, D flat, G flat, C flat.

Review Exercises

1. Fill in the blanks:

a)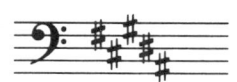

The above key signature for the scale of ____ major shows us that the notes ____ ____ ____ ____ ____ are to be played _____.

b)

The above key signature for the scale of ____ major shows us that the notes ____ ____ ____ ____ ____ ____ are to be played _____.

c)

The above key signature for the scale of ____ major shows us that the notes ____ ____ ____ ____ ____ ____ ____ are to be played _____.

2. Name the major scales these key signatures represent:

____ Major   ____ Major   ____ Major

   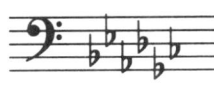   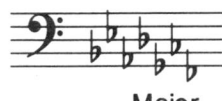

____ Major   ____ Major   ____ Major

Grouping of Sharps and Flats in a Key Signature

This is the order in which the sharps are written in the treble and bass clefs. Write the names of the sharps on the lines below the staves.

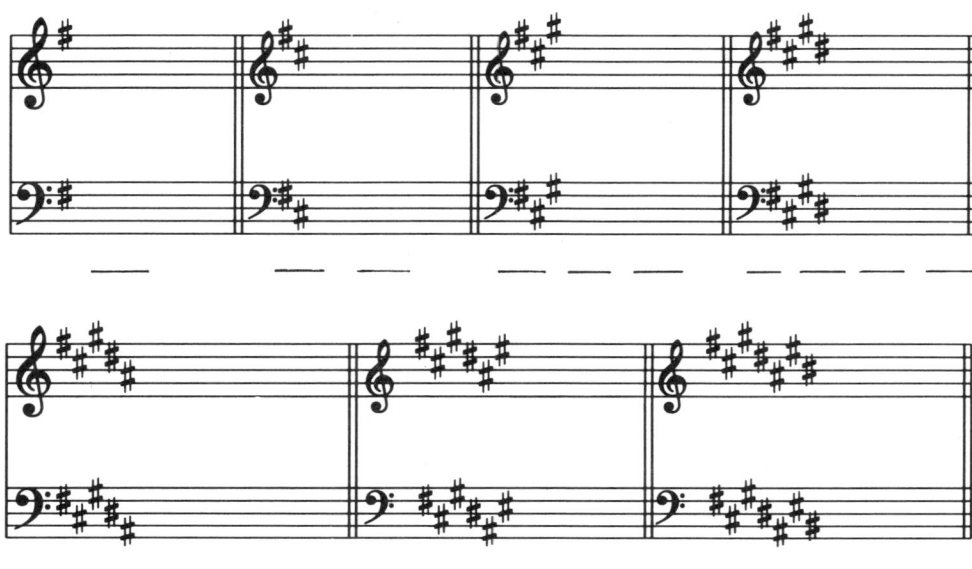

This is the order in which the flats are written in the treble and bass clefs. Write the names of the flats on the lines below the staves.

Review Exercises

1a. Practice writing the sharps on the staff in their correct order in the extra bars provided.

b. Write the name of the sharps below the staff.

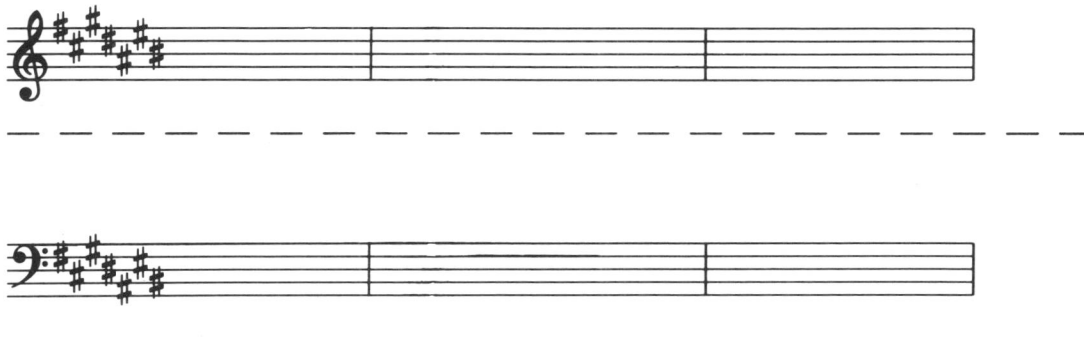

2a. Practice writing the flats on the staff in their correct order in the extra bars provided.

b. Write the names of the flats below the staff.

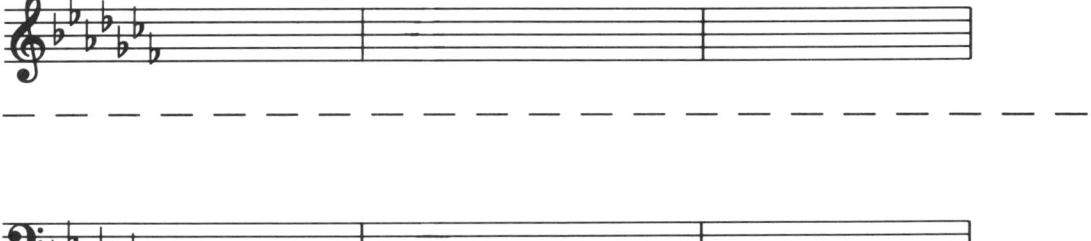

Summary

1. _____, _____, _____, _____ _____, and _____ _____ are called accidentals.

2. Notes temporarily altered by accidentals remain changed for a measure, unless altered by another_____ or_____into the next measure.

3. A double sharp (×) means that the note is to be played a_____ _____ higher.

4. All accidentals are written on the_____ side of the note on the staff and on the_____ side of the letter name of the note.

5. A double flat (♭♭) means that the note is to be played a_____ _____ lower.

6. Write the ascending order of technical names for the notes of any scale:
   _____ _____ _____ _____
   _____ _____ _____

7. The order of tones and semitones in the major scale is as follows:
   ___ ___ ___ ___ ___ ___ ___

8. Write the order of sharps: _____ _____ _____ _____ _____ _____ _____

9. Write the order of flats: _____ _____ _____ _____ _____ _____ _____

Perfect Score: 41   Student's Score:

Review Exercise

1a. Name the key of each of the following scales with the tonic note given (1 mark).

b. Using accidentals instead of a key signature, write each scale ascending and descending (1 mark).

c. Mark and label the tones and semitones (1 mark).

Key _____ Major

_____ Major

_____ Major

_____ Major

_____ Major

_____ Major

_____ Major

_____ Major

_____ Major

2. First write the key signature, then use whole notes to write the following major scales in ascending order (3 marks).

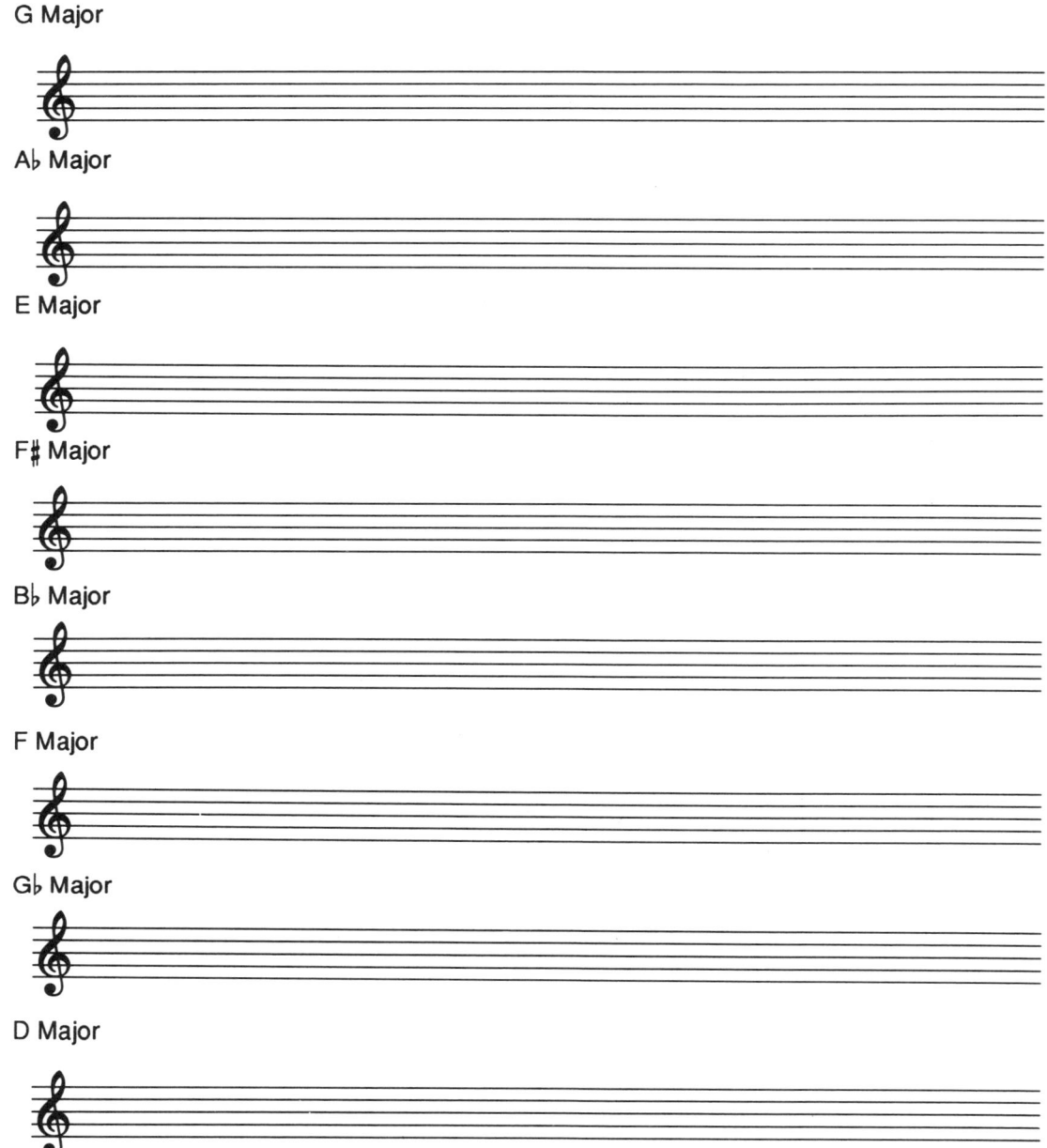

G Major

A♭ Major

E Major

F♯ Major

B♭ Major

F Major

G♭ Major

D Major

Perfect Score: 24   Student's Score:

3. First write the key signature, then use sixteenth notes to write the following major scales in descending order (3 marks).

E Major

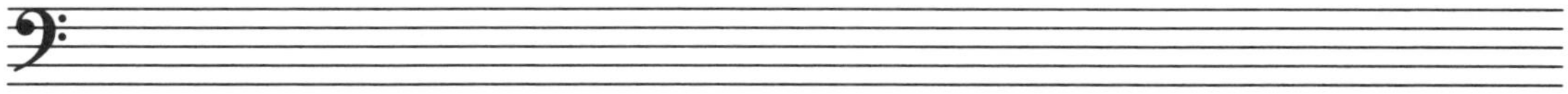

A Major

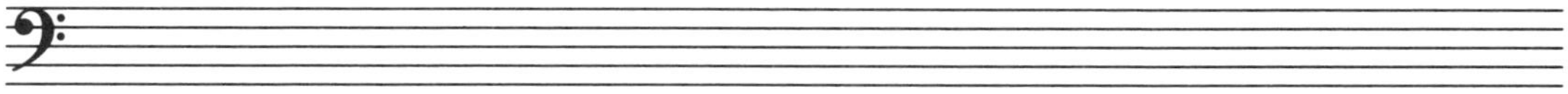

Cb Major

Db Major

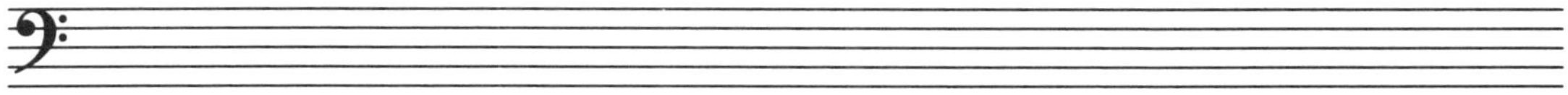

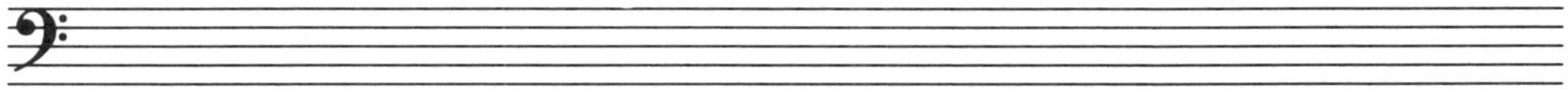

B Major

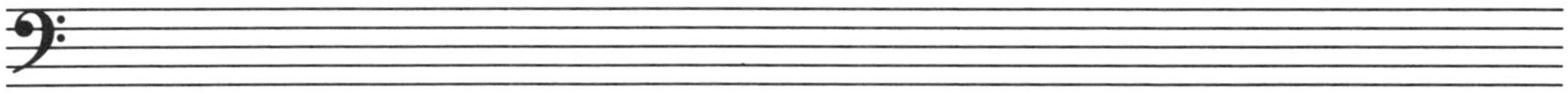

C# Major

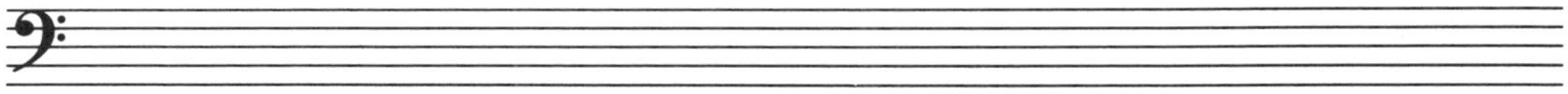

Gb Major

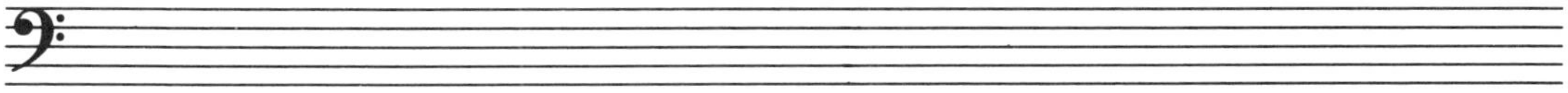

C Major

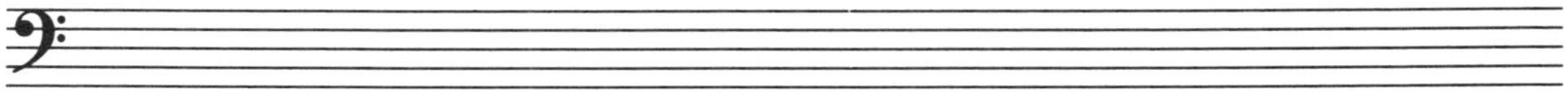

Perfect Score: 24   Student's Score:

4a. Name the key (1 mark).

b. Write the following notes in the given clef (1 mark).

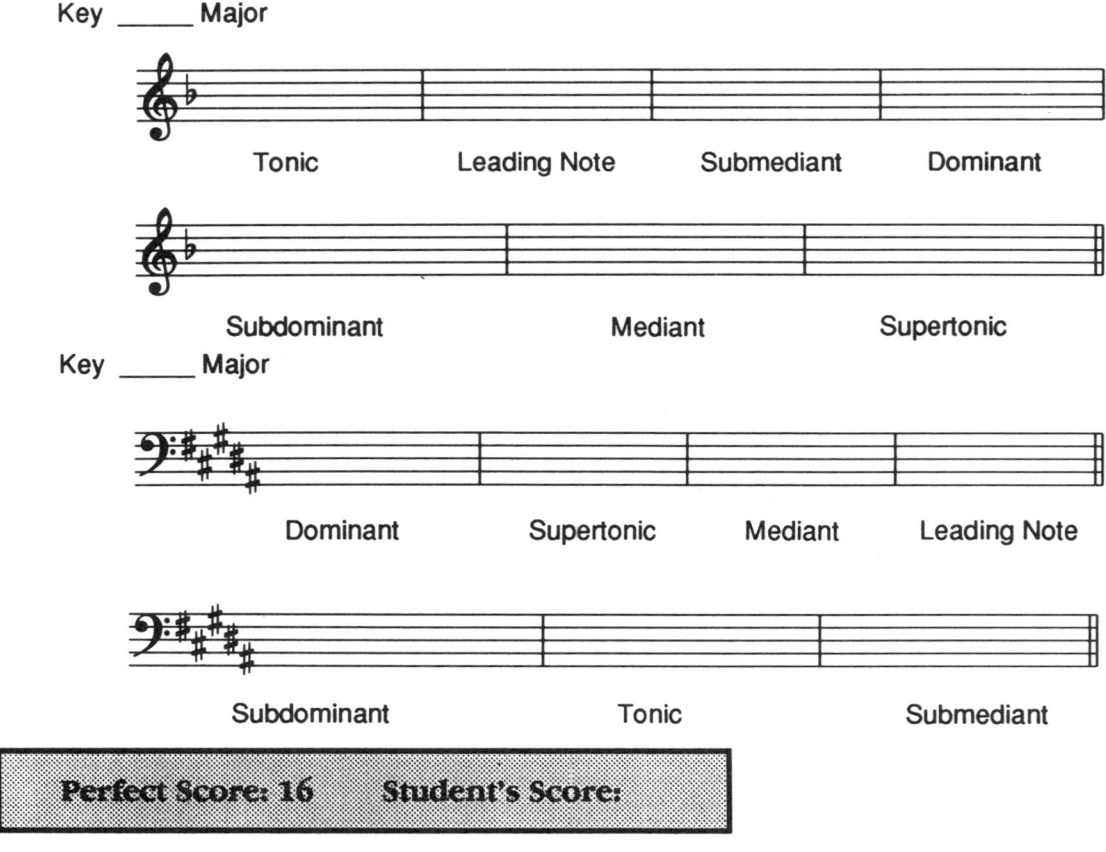

5. Below each of the following notes write:

a) the name of the **major** key (1 mark)

b) the degree (technical) name of the note in the scale (1 mark)

6. Using the correct key signature, write the following notes on the staff and write the degree (technical) name of the note on the line below the staff (2 marks).

a) the first note of D major

b) the fifth note of B flat major

c) the second note of E flat major

d) the sixth note of C sharp major

e) the fourth note of F major

f) the seventh note of G major

g) the third note of C major

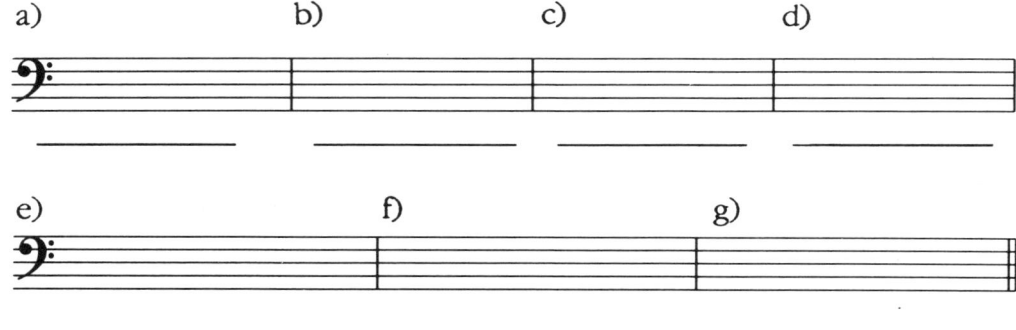

Perfect Score: 14   Student's Score:

7. Using accidentals instead of a key signature, write the following notes (1 mark):

a) the leading note of F sharp major

b) the supertonic of A major

c) the dominant of C flat major

d) the mediant of D flat major

e) the subdominant of E major

f) the submediant of G flat major

g) the tonic of A flat major

h) the mediant of B major

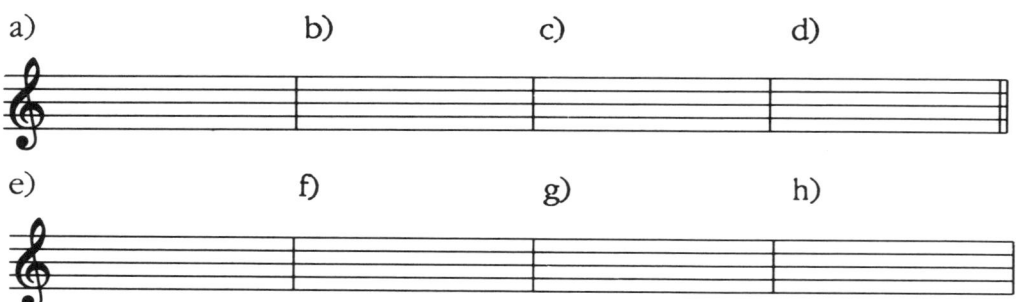

Perfect Score: 8   Student's Score:

8. Write the following scales ascending and descending using the **correct key signature** (2 marks).

  a) F major from supertonic to supertonic

  b) B major from dominant to dominant

  c) D flat major from leading note to leading note

  d) A major from submediant to submediant

  e) F sharp major from mediant to mediant

  f) G flat major from subdominant to subdominant

  g) D major from tonic to tonic

Perfect Score: 14   Student's Score:

9. Write the following key signatures:

a) in the treble clef (1 mark)

G Major	Ab Major	Eb Major	F Major	D Major	Bb Major	A Major

b) in the bass clef (1 mark)

E Major	Db Major	B Major	Cb Major	F# Major	Gb Major	A Major

Perfect Score: 14   Student's Score:

Minor Scales

Harmonic Minor Scales
Written and Keyboard (optional) Exercise

(It is recommended that these be done at the keyboard where the student can see the notes and listen to the sounds.)

In the harmonic minor scales below:

a) Name the key (1 mark).

b) Mark the tone $\sqcap$ (T), semitone $\sqcap$ (S), and tone-plus-semitone $\sqcap\sqcap$ (T+S) intervals in the following scales, adding accidentals (flats, naturals, etc.) where necessary (7 marks).

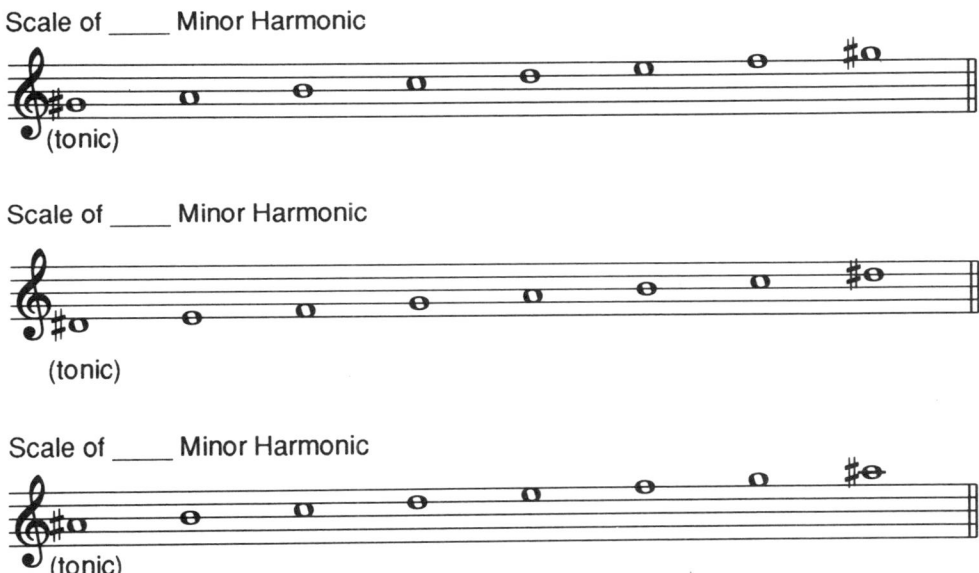

Scale of ____ Minor Harmonic (tonic)

Scale of ____ Minor Harmonic (tonic)

Scale of ____ Minor Harmonic (tonic)

| Perfect Score: 24 | Student's Score: |

Keyboard Exercise (optional)

Play each of these harmonic minor scales: A, E, B, F♯, C♯, G♯, D♯, A♯.

Written Exercise

In the harmonic minor scales below:

a) Name the key (1 mark).

b) Mark the tone, semitone, and tone-plus-semitone intervals in the following scales, adding accidentals (flats, naturals, etc.) where necessary (7 marks).

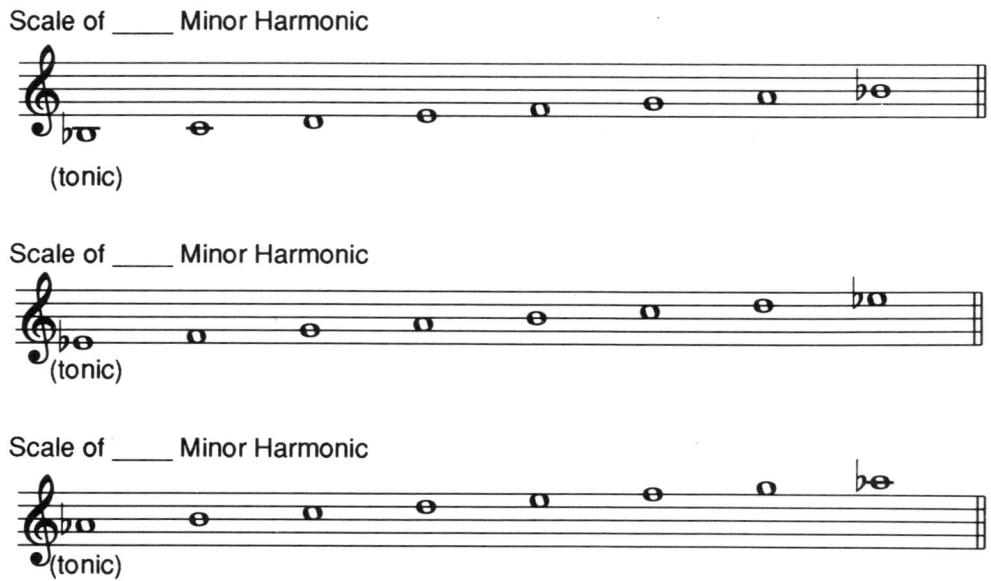

Scale of _____ Minor Harmonic

(tonic)

Scale of _____ Minor Harmonic

(tonic)

Scale of _____ Minor Harmonic

(tonic)

Perfect Score: 24   Student's Score:

Keyboard Exercise (optional)

Play each of these harmonic minor scales: D, G, C, F, B♭, E♭, A♭.

Melodic Minor Scales
Written and Keyboard (optional) Exercise

(It is recommended that these be done at the keyboard where the student can see the notes and listen to the sounds.)

In the melodic minor scales below:

a) Name the key (1 mark).

b) Mark the tone, semitone intervals in the following scales, adding accidentals (sharps, double sharps, naturals) where necessary (14 marks).

The order of tones, semitones, etc., is as follows in the melodic minor scale:

Ascending: T, S, T, T, T, T, S,

Descending: T, T, S, T, T, S, T.

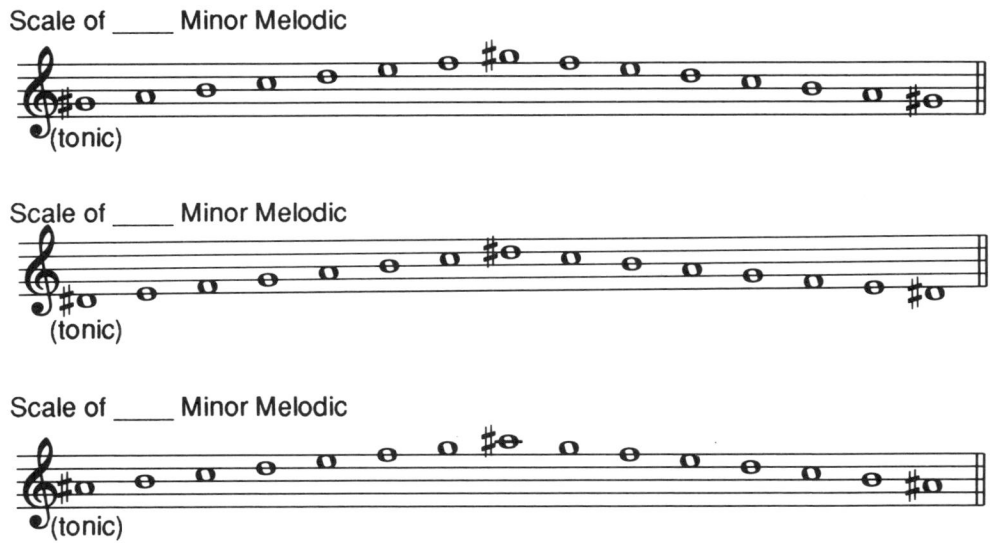

Scale of _____ Minor Melodic

(tonic)

Scale of _____ Minor Melodic

(tonic)

Scale of _____ Minor Melodic

(tonic)

Perfect Score: 45   Student's Score:

Keyboard Exercises (optional)

Play each of these melodic minor scales: A, E, B, F♯, C♯, G♯, D♯, A♯.

Written Exercises

In the melodic minor scales below a) name the key (1 mark), and b) mark the tone and semitone intervals in the following scales, adding accidentals (flats, naturals) where necessary (14 marks).

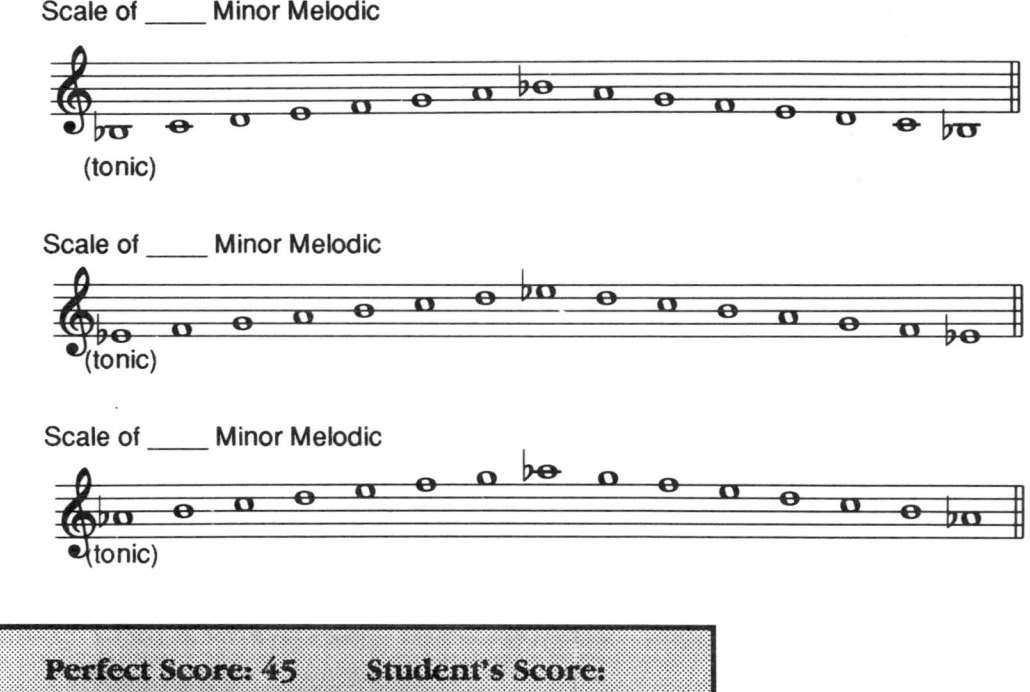

Scale of _____ Minor Melodic

(tonic)

Scale of _____ Minor Melodic

(tonic)

Scale of _____ Minor Melodic

(tonic)

Perfect Score: 45   Student's Score:

Keyboard Exercise (optional)

Play each of these melodic minor scales: D, G, C, F, B♭, E♭, A♭.

Written Exercise

Fill in the blanks with a) the major key name (1 mark), and b) the relative minor key (1 mark).

Major Key C _____ _____ _____ _____ _____ _____

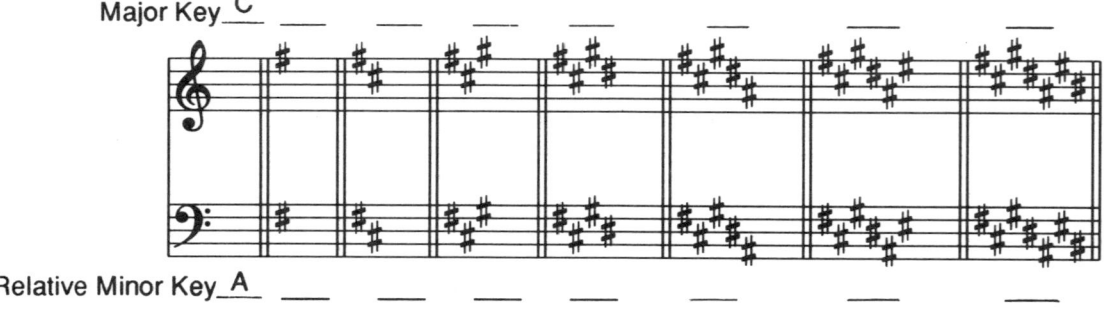

Relative Minor Key A _____ _____ _____ _____ _____ _____

Major Key___ ___ ___ ___ ___ ___ ___

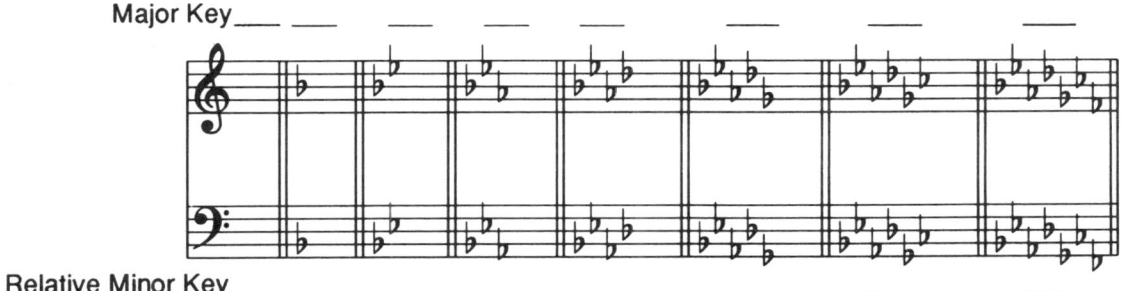

Relative Minor Key___ ___ ___ ___ ___ ___ ___

Perfect Score: 30   Student's Score:

Review Exercise

1. Write the following minor scales in the treble clef, ascending and descending, using accidentals instead of key signatures (3 marks). Name the key of each scale (1 mark).

Key ____ Minor Harmonic

Key ____ Minor Melodic

Key ____ Minor Harmonic

Key ____ Minor Harmonic

Key ____ Minor Melodic

Perfect Score: 20   Student's Score:

2. Write the following minor scales in the bass clef, ascending and descending, using the correct key signatures (3 marks). Name the key of each scale (1 mark).

Key ____ Minor Harmonic

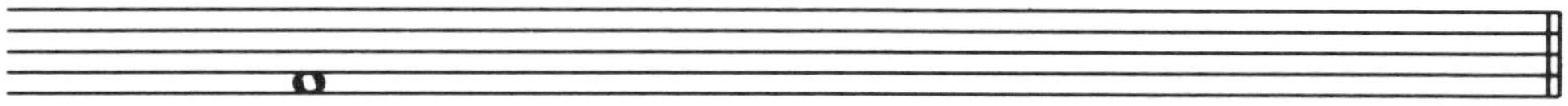

Key ____ Minor Harmonic

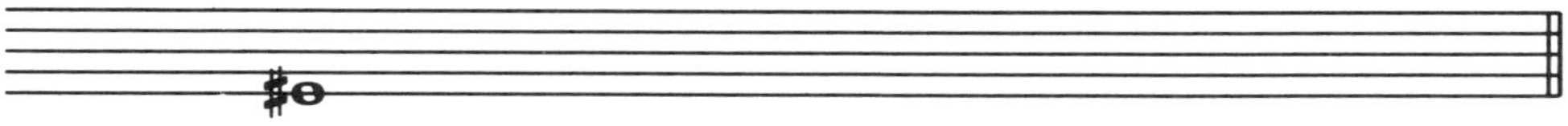

Key ____ Minor Melodic

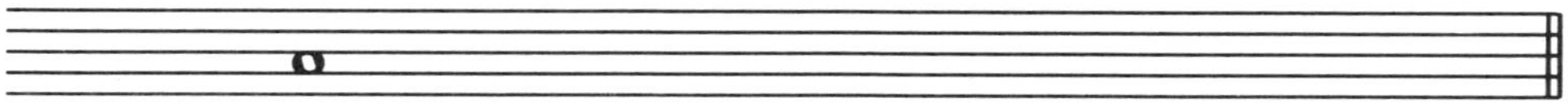

Key ____ Minor Melodic

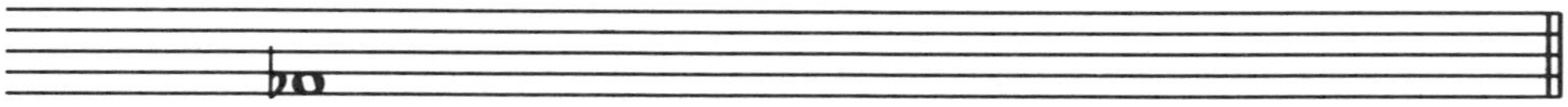

Key ____ Minor Harmonic

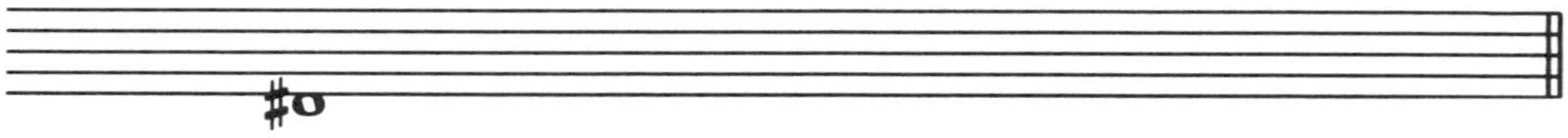

Perfect Score: 20   Student's Score:

3. Write the following minor scales, ascending and descending, in the treble clef using the correct key signatures (3 marks). Mark the tones T, semitones S, and the tone-plus-semitone T+S intervals (1 mark).

E Minor Harmonic

F Minor Harmonic

A♯ Minor Melodic

D♯ Minor Harmonic

B♭ Minor Melodic

Perfect Score: 20   Student's Score:

4. Write the following scales, ascending and descending, in the bass clef using the correct key signatures (3 marks).

D Major

The Relative Minor Harmonic of D Major

The Tonic Minor Melodic of D Major

Perfect Score: 9   Student's Score:

5. Write the following scales in the treble clef, ascending and descending, using accidentals instead of a key signature (3 marks).

E Flat Major

The Relative Minor Melodic of E Flat Major

The Tonic Minor Harmonic of E Flat Major

Perfect Score: 9   Student's Score:

6. Write the following minor scales in the treble clef, ascending and descending, using the correct key signatures (3 marks).

F Minor Melodic from Dominant to Dominant

The Harmonic Minor from Tonic to Tonic Whose Leading Note Is B Sharp

B Minor Harmonic from Mediant to Mediant

The Melodic Minor from Tonic to Tonic Whose Subdominant Is F

Perfect Score: 12   Student's Score:

7. Write the key signatures of the following keys (1 mark):

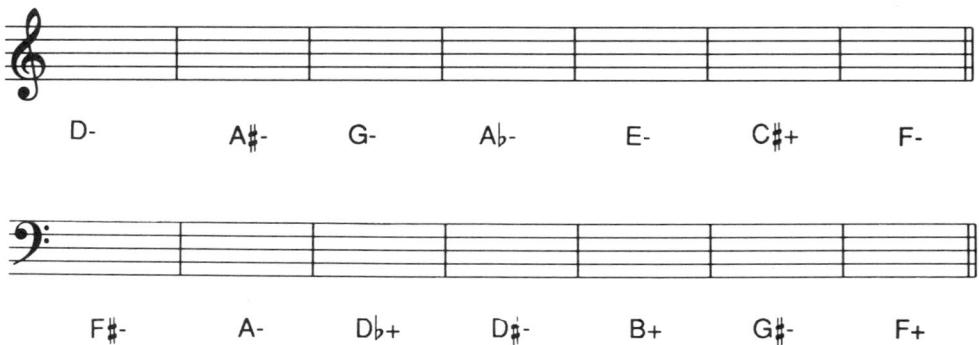

D-   A♯-   G-   A♭-   E-   C♯+   F-

F♯-   A-   D♭+   D♯-   B+   G♯-   F+

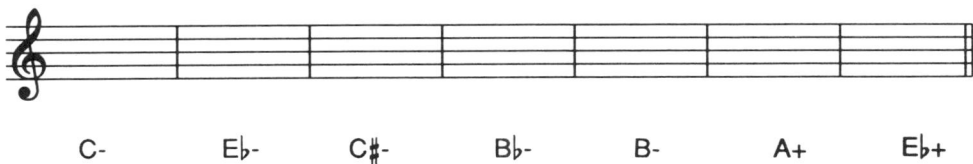

C-   E♭-   C♯-   B♭-   B-   A+   E♭+

Perfect Score: 21   Student's Score:

8. Add the proper clefs, key signatures and accidentals where necessary to form the following scales (3 marks).

F Sharp Minor Harmonic

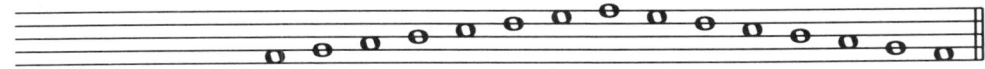

D Flat Major

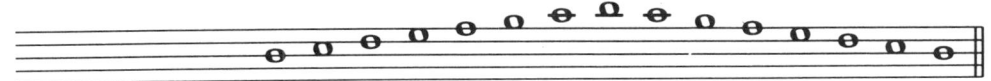

B Flat Minor Melodic

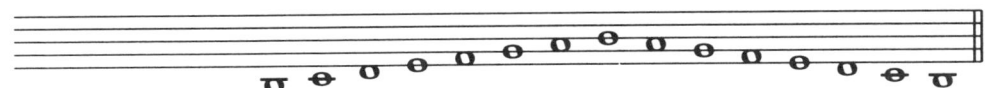

E Minor Harmonic

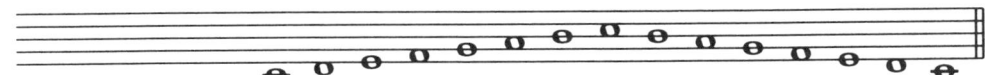

Perfect Score: 12   Student's Score:

Compound Time

A Special Word About Compound Time

This area of study is often least understood by many students. The problem seems to be in understanding the difference between beats and pulses. We hope the following explanation will be helpful.

In compound time, notes are grouped in three-beat patterns called **pulses.**

Compare $\frac{2}{4}$ and $\frac{6}{8}$ time.

In $\frac{2}{4}$ time there are two beats or pulses in a bar, and in $\frac{6}{8}$ time there are six beats or two pulses (that is, two groups of three beats) in a bar.

Keyboard Exercise (optional)

Teacher: Ask the student to clap and play the rhythm of each following exercise to feel the pulses in each bar.

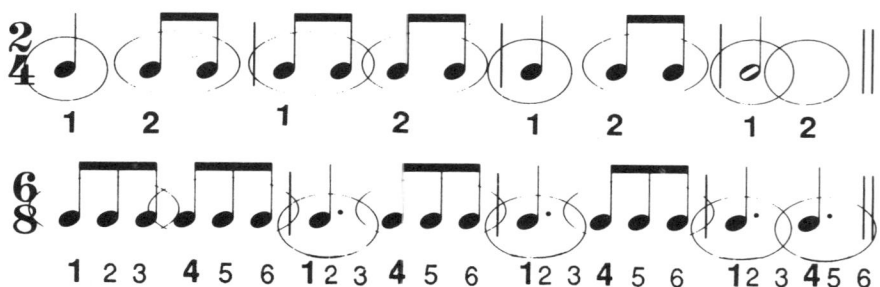

Compare $\frac{3}{4}$ and $\frac{9}{8}$ time.

In $\frac{3}{4}$ time there are three beats or pulses in a bar, and in $\frac{9}{8}$ time there are nine beats or three pulses (that is, three groups of three beats) in a bar.

Keyboard Exercise (optional)

Teacher: Ask the student to clap and play the rhythm of each exercise below to feel the pulse in each bar.

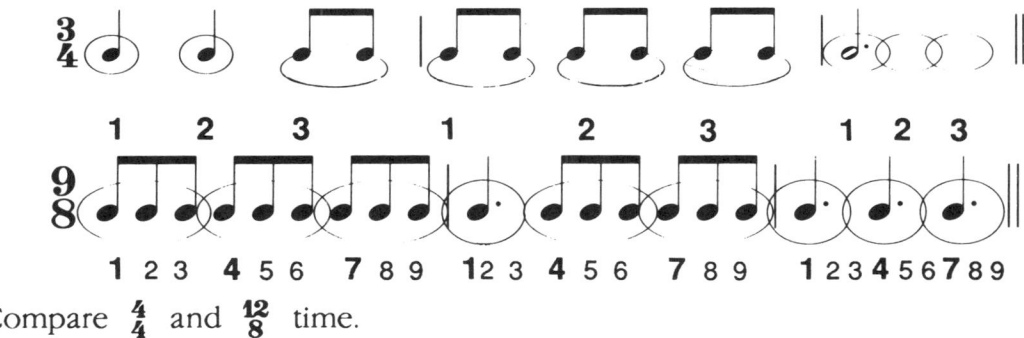

Compare $\frac{4}{4}$ and $\frac{12}{8}$ time.

In $\frac{4}{4}$ time there are four beats or pulses in a bar, and in $\frac{12}{8}$ time there are twelve beats or four pulses (that is, four groups of three beats) in a bar.

Keyboard Exercise (optional)

Teacher: Ask the student to clap and play (any note) the rhythm of each exercise below to feel the pulse in each bar.

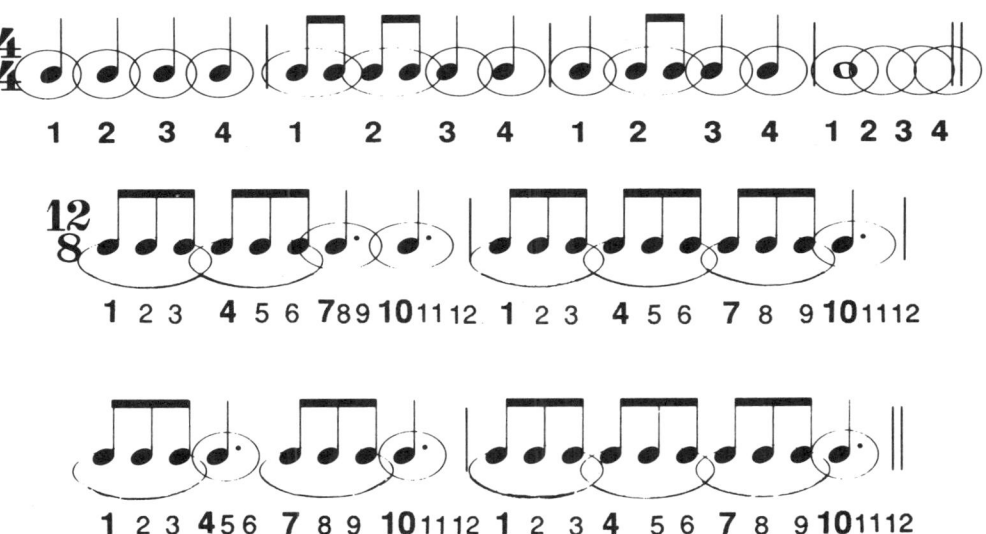

Written Exercises

1. The most commonly used compound time signatures with two groups of three-beat rhythmic patterns:

a)

In $\frac{6}{8}$ time there are _____ beats and _____ pulses in each bar.

b)

In $\frac{6}{16}$ time there are _____ beats and _____ pulses in each bar.

c)

In $\frac{6}{4}$ time there are _____ beats and _____ pulses in each bar.

2. The most commonly used time signatures with three groups of three-beat rhythmic patterns:

a)

In $\frac{9}{8}$ time there are _____ beats and _____ pulses in each bar.

b)

In $\frac{9}{16}$ time there are _____ beats and _____ pulses in each bar.

c)

In $\frac{9}{4}$ time there are ____ beats and ____ pulses in each bar.

3. The most commonly used time signatures with four groups of three-beat rhythmic patterns:

a)

In $\frac{12}{8}$ time there are ____ beats and ____ pulses in each bar.

b)

In $\frac{12}{16}$ time there are ____ beats and ____ pulses in each bar.

c)

In $\frac{12}{4}$ time there are ____ beats and ____ pulses in each bar.

Perfect Score: 18   Student's Score:

Grouping Notes in Compound Time
Written and Keyboard (optional) Exercises

In each of the following melodies:

a) circle the groups of three-beat pulses (1 mark each)

b) play the melody

c) clap the rhythmic pattern, counting aloud

16 marks 5.

8 marks 6.

Perfect Score: 72   Student's Score:

Grouping of Rests in Compound Time

It is important that rests clearly show beats in music.

In compound time, notes are grouped in three-beat patterns, and rests must always be written in place of or to complete a three-beat grouping.

1. To complete the first two beats of a three-beat note grouping in compound time, use one rest.

e.g.,

2. To complete the last two beats of a three-beat note grouping in compound time, use two rests.

e.g.,

3. To complete the first or last half of a bar having twelve beats (e.g., $\frac{12}{8}$, $\frac{12}{4}$, $\frac{12}{16}$), use one dotted rest.

e.g.,

Here are some other groupings of notes and rests:

One whole-note rest is used to indicate a complete measure (bar) of silence in any time signature.

e.g.,

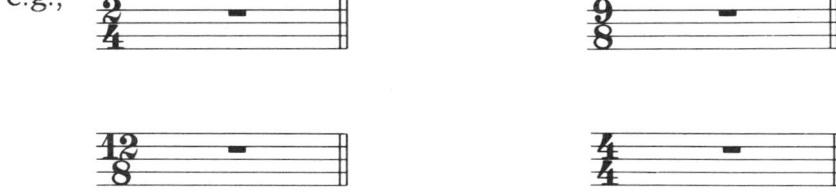

Irregular Time Signatures

Time signatures with five or seven beats within a bar are frequently used in twentieth century music.

Clap the following rhythms, noting the irregular accents.

Complete the sentences beside each example.

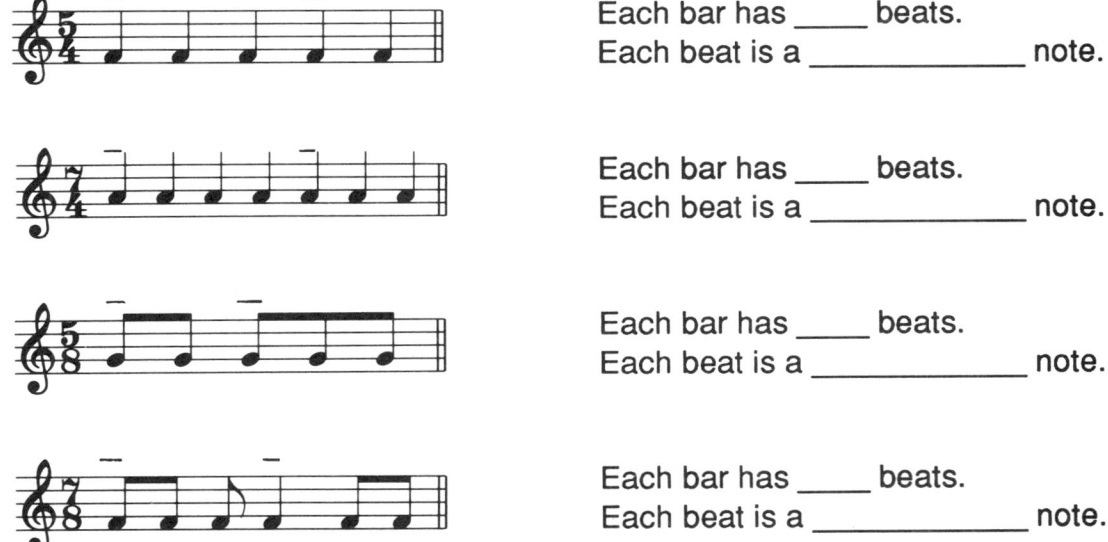

Each bar has _____ beats.
Each beat is a _____ note.

Each bar has _____ beats.
Each beat is a _____ note.

Each bar has _____ beats.
Each beat is a _____ note.

Each bar has _____ beats.
Each beat is a _____ note.

Syncopation

To introduce rhythmic variety into music, the composer sometimes makes use of a device called **syncopation. Syncopation** is the temporary changing of the natural *accent* from a weak beat to a strong beat.

The circled notes indicate several kinds of syncopation.

Clap the following rhythmic patterns, noting the accentuation in each.

a)

Usual
Syncopation

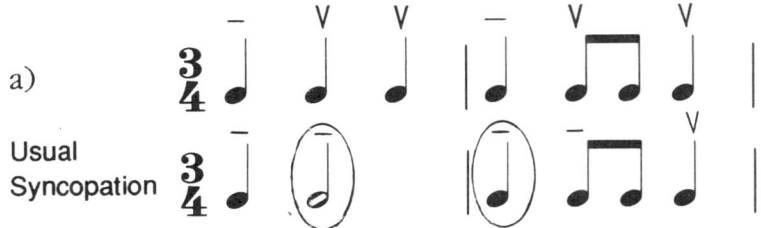

Usual syncopation occurs when a naturally weak beat is made strong by adding an accent, thereby temporarily changing the regular rhythm.

b)

Natural
Syncopation

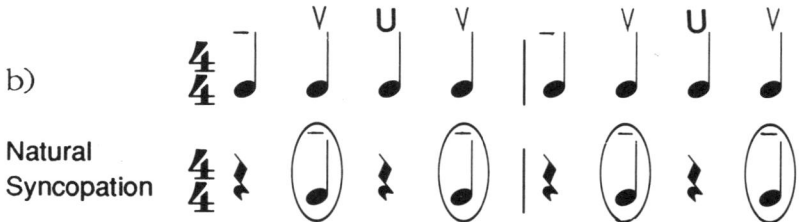

Natural syncopation occurs on a note following a rest because this note becomes automatically accented, creating a temporary change in the regular rhythm.

c)

Natural
Syncopation

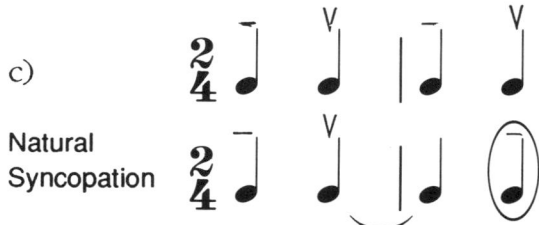

Natural syncopation occurs on a note following a tie because this note becomes automatically accented, creating a temporary change in the regular rhythm.

Remember: — strong; V weak; U medium, which indicate accentuation.

Keyboard Exercise (optional)

Play the following and take note of the examples of the syncopation

Irregular Note Groups

Sometimes it is necessary for composers to write more or fewer notes in a bar than the time signature allows.

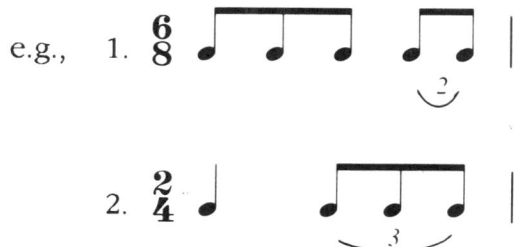

A slur and a number are written above or below a group of the same kind of notes (e.g., eighth notes above) to indicate that an adjustment in total time value of each group has to be made.

This adjustment is made according to whether the time value of the note group has to be lengthened or shortened by the time remaining in the bar, e.g.,

1. The time of the group of two eighth notes above has to be adjusted in order to be played in the time of three eighth notes necessary to complete the remaining time value of the bar.

2. The time of the group of three eighth notes above has to be adjusted in order to be played in the time of two eighth notes necessary to complete the remaining time value of the bar.

Here are some examples of irregular note groups which have to be adjusted to fit the time signature.

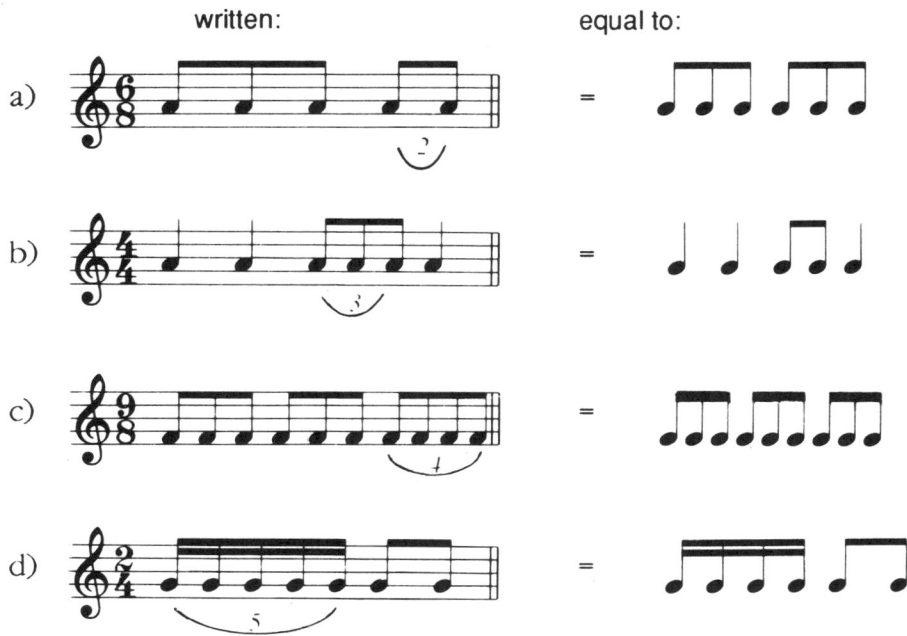

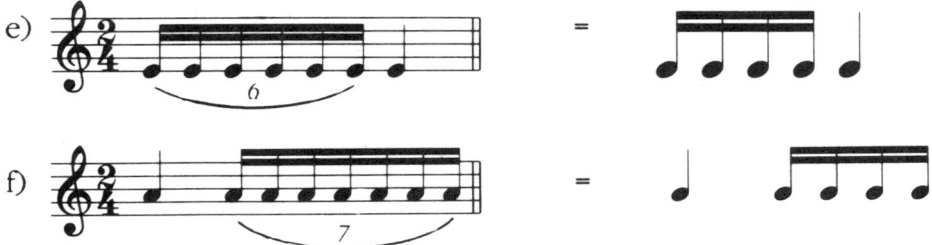

Written Exercise

Fill in the time signatures of each of the following bars and write the equivalent notation in the space provided (2 marks).

Review Exercises

1. Complete the following by adding rests within the brackets (1 mark per bracket).

Perfect Score: 56   Student's Score:

2. Divide each of the following series of notes into two bars (1 mark) and insert the time signature (1 mark).

Perfect Score: 22   Student's Score:

3. Complete the following lines of music by adding another two bars in the given time signature (2 marks).

Write a simple melody using the same rhythmic pattern (4 marks). Play your melody.

Example:

a)

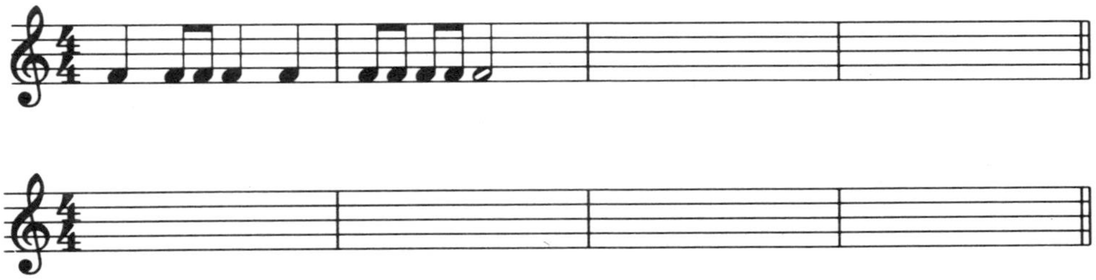

b)

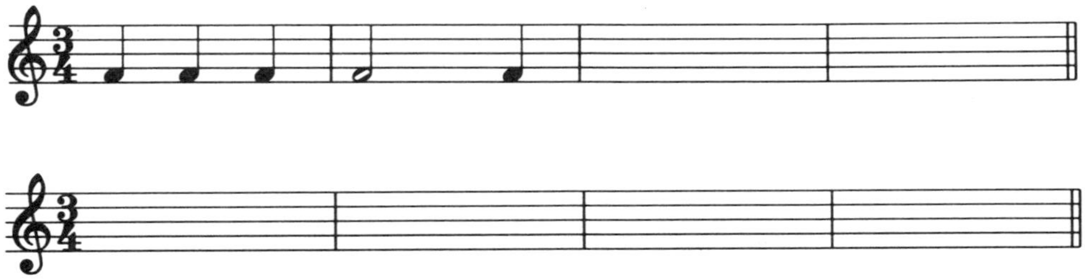

c)

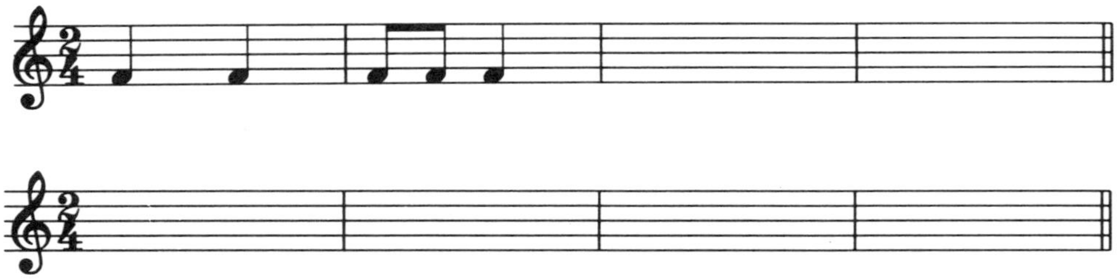

d)

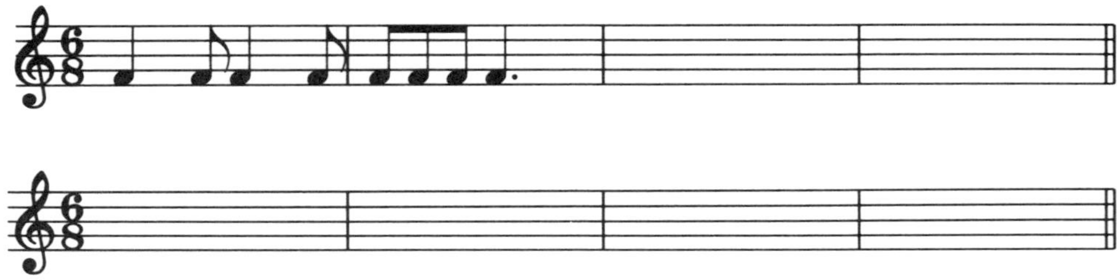

Perfect Score: 24 **Student's Score:**

4. Complete the following lines of music by adding another two bars in the given time signature (2 marks). Clap the four-bar rhythmic pattern.

a)

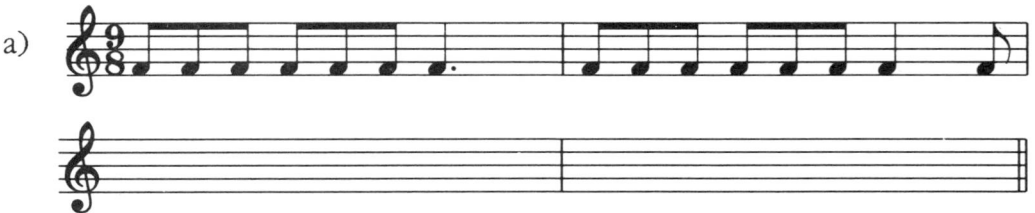

Perfect Score: 10   Student's Score:

Keyboard Exercises (optional)

Each of the following excerpts has no time signature indicated. Play each of the excerpts twice and insert the correct time signature.

Minuet

Grazioso

J. S. Bach

1.

Sonatina

Allegretto   L. van Beethoven

2.

Sonatina

Moderato   F. le Couppey

3.

Sonatina

Vivace   Clementi

4.

Air

Andante

J. G. Graeff

5.

Allegretto

Hunter

6.

Aria

Moderato

J. S. Bach

7.

Musette in D

Allegro con brio

J. S. Bach

8.

Passepied

Andantino   Couperin

9.

Chorale

Andante   J. S. Bach

10.

Review

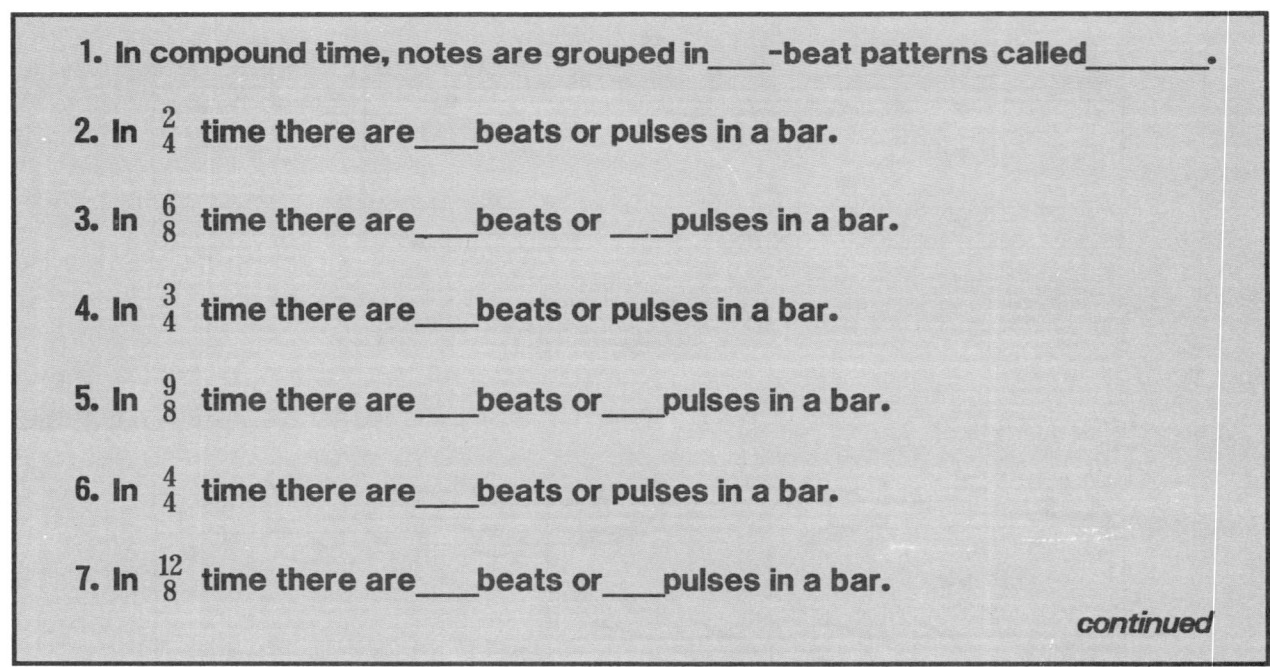

1. In compound time, notes are grouped in____-beat patterns called_____.

2. In $\frac{2}{4}$ time there are____beats or pulses in a bar.

3. In $\frac{6}{8}$ time there are____beats or ____pulses in a bar.

4. In $\frac{3}{4}$ time there are____beats or pulses in a bar.

5. In $\frac{9}{8}$ time there are____beats or____pulses in a bar.

6. In $\frac{4}{4}$ time there are____beats or pulses in a bar.

7. In $\frac{12}{8}$ time there are____beats or____pulses in a bar.

continued

8. The most commonly used compound time signatures are:

$\frac{6}{8}$ and____and____.

$\frac{9}{8}$ and____and____.

$\frac{12}{8}$ and____and____.

9. In compound time, notes are grouped in three beat patterns, and rests must always be written in place of or to_____a three-beat grouping.

10. To complete the first two beats of a three-beat note grouping in compound time, use____rest(s).

11. To complete the last two beats of a three-beat note grouping in compound time, use____rest(s).

12. To complete the first or last half of a bar having twelve beats, use_____rest(s).

13. The_____-_____rest is used to indicate a complete measure of silence in any time signature.

14. Give examples of four irregular time signatures. ____ ____ ____ ____

15. Usual syncopation occurs when a naturally_____beat is made strong by adding an accent, thereby temporarily changing the regular rhythm.

16. Natural syncopation occurs on a note_____a rest because this note becomes automatically accented, creating a temporary change in the regular rhythm.

17. Natural syncopation occurs on a note_____a tie because this note becomes automatically accented, creating a temporary change in the regular rhythm.

18. A_____and a_____are written above or below a grouping of the same kind of notes to indicate an adjustment in total time value which must be made for it to agree with the time signature.

Perfect Score: 33   Student's Score:

Intervals

An interval is the distance or difference in pitch between any two notes.

Naming Intervals of Notes in the Major Scales

Here are the intervals built on the keynote of the scale of F major:

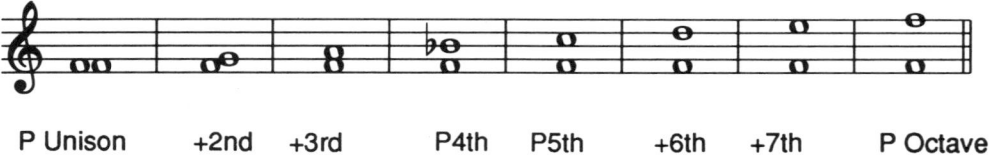

| P Unison | +2nd | +3rd | P4th | P5th | +6th | +7th | P Octave |

In all major scales, **perfect** intervals always occur on the unison, fourth, fifth and octave degrees of the scale.

In all major scales, **major** intervals always occur on the second, third, sixth and seventh degrees of the scale.

Remember that the bottom note of an interval is the keynote or tonic of the major scale, and notes within the scale form either perfect or major intervals from the keynote

Naming Intervals of Notes Not in the Major Scales

Minor intervals are written a semitone lower than major intervals. The upper note is not found in the major scale of the keynote.

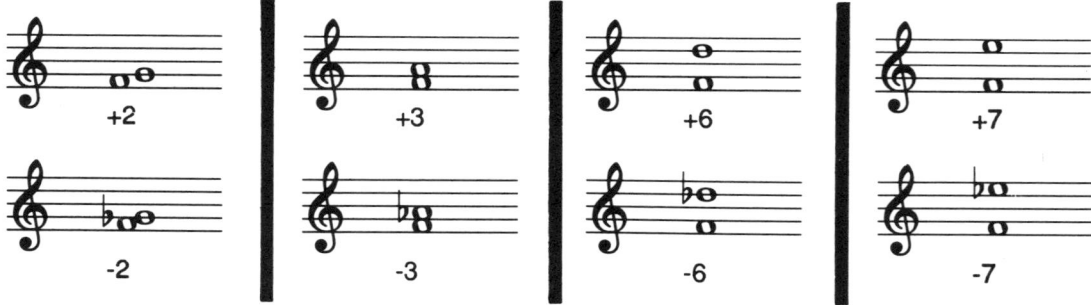

More Intervals —
The Augmented and Diminished Intervals

When a perfect or major interval is made a semitone larger, it is called an **augmented** interval (abbreviation "X").

The upper note of an augmented interval is not found in the major scale of the keynote.

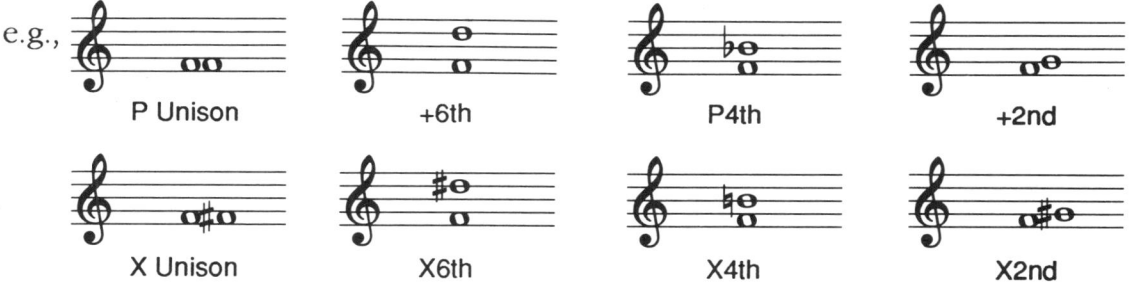

When a **perfect** or **minor** interval is made a semitone smaller, it is called a **diminished** interval (abbreviation "O").

The upper note of a diminished interval is not found in the major scale of the keynote.

Keyboard Exercise (optional)

At the keyboard, change the following **perfect** or **major** intervals to **augmented** intervals by making each a semitone larger.

At the keyboard, change the following **perfect** or **minor** intervals to **diminished** intervals by making each a semitone smaller.

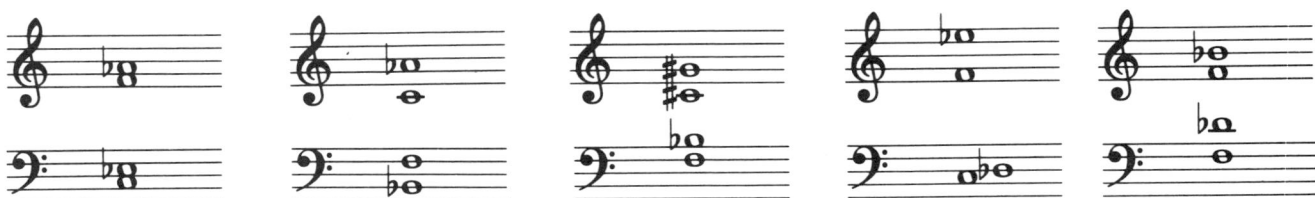

At times, students are required to name an interval whose keynote is not the first note of any major scale.

e.g.,

There is no G sharp major scale.

The solution to naming an interval such as the one above must be carefully thought out in the following manner:

1. Omit the sharp from the lower note and consider G to be the keynote of the major scale.

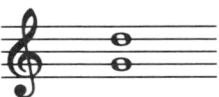

2. The interval from G to D is a P5th for the upper note D, found in the major scale of the lower note.

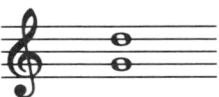

3. Replace the sharp on the lower note, making the P5th interval a semitone smaller; therefore, the interval becomes that of a diminished 5th.

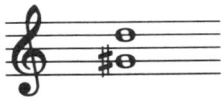

The interval, therefore, is a O5th.

Written Exercise

Using the solution just suggested, name the intervals given below:

_____   _____   _____   _____

Written Exercise

1. Write an augmented unison *beside* each of the given notes (6 marks).

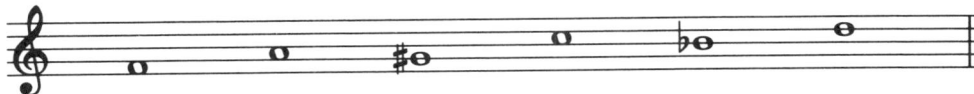

2. Write an augmented second *above* each of the given notes (6 marks).

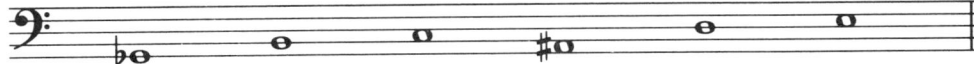

3. Write an augmented fourth *above* each of the given notes (6 marks).

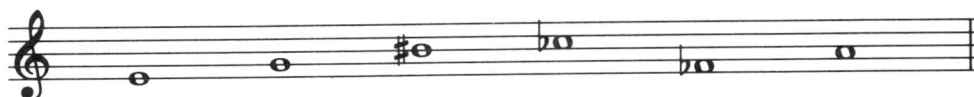

4. Write an augmented fifth *above* each of the given notes (6 marks).

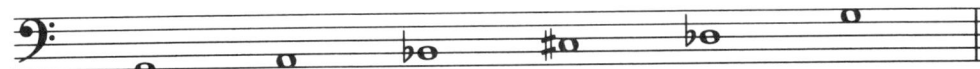

5. Write an augmented sixth *above* each of the given notes (6 marks).

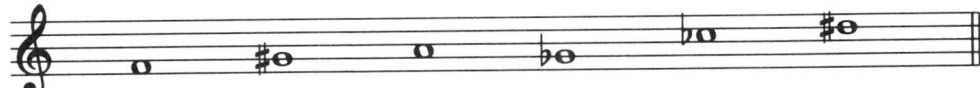

6. Write an augmented seventh *above* each of the given notes (6 marks).

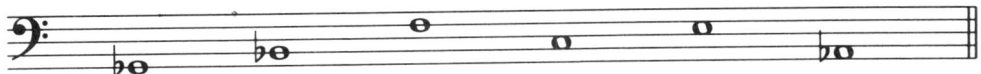

7. Write an diminished second *above* each of the given notes (6 marks).

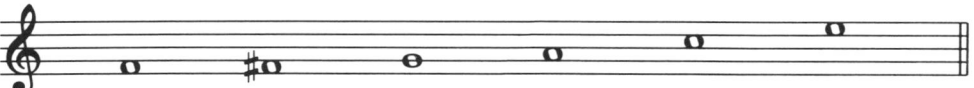

8. Write a diminished third *above* each of the given notes (6 marks).

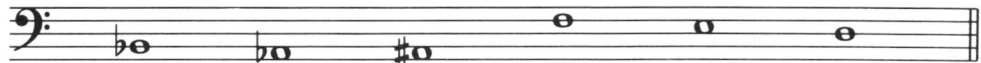

9. Write a diminished fourth *above* each of the given notes. (6 marks).

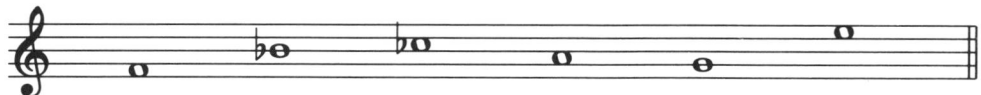

10. Write a diminished fifth *above* each of the given notes (6 marks).

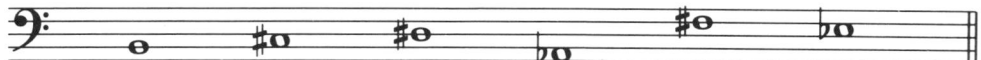

11. Write a diminished sixth *above* each of the given notes (6 marks).

12. Write a diminished seventh *above* each of the given notes (6 marks).

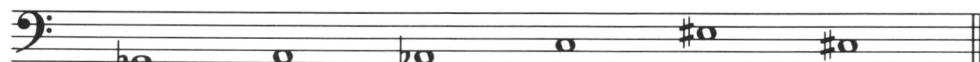

Perfect Score: 72   Student's Score:

Inversion of Intervals

To invert an interval you write the lower note an octave higher,

e.g.,

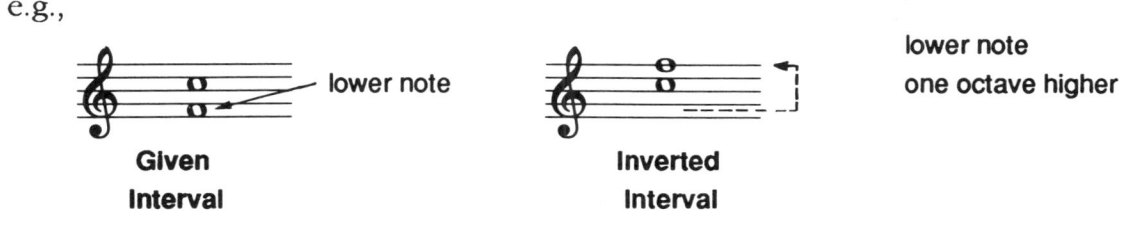

OR

you write the higher note an octave lower,

e.g.,

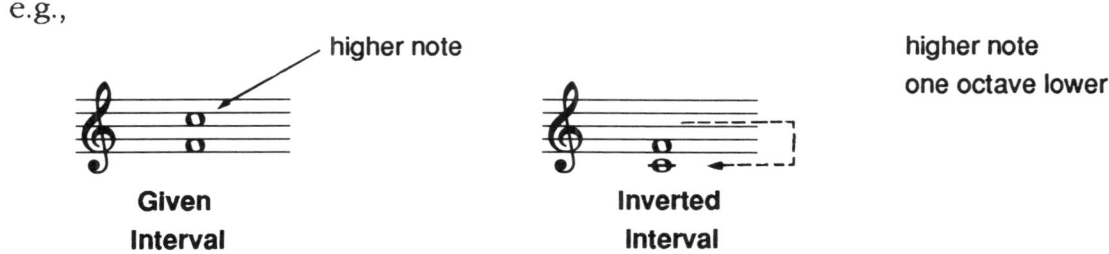

Keyboard Exercise (optional)

Invert each of the following intervals by playing the lower note an octave higher (play the given interval first, then the inverted interval).

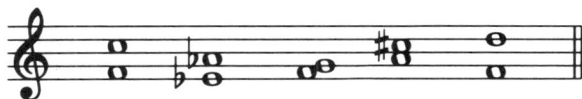

Invert each of the following intervals by playing the higher note an octave lower (play the given interval first, then the inverted interval).

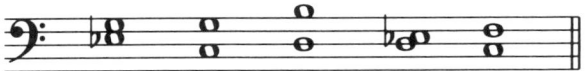

When intervals are inverted, both the numerical distance and the interval name change.

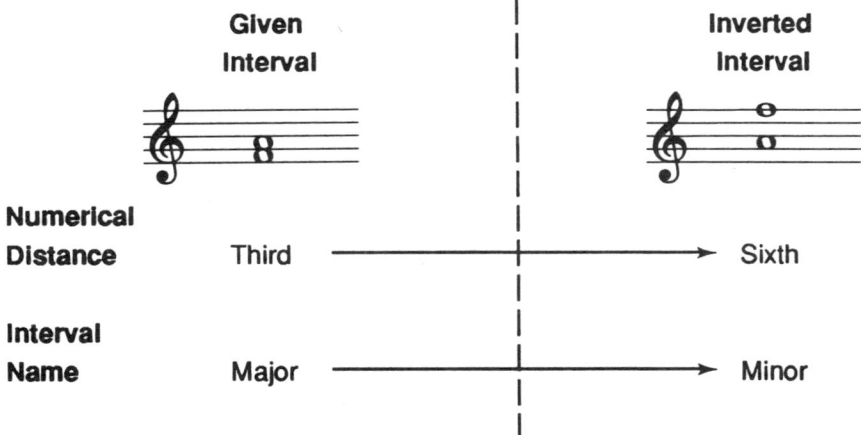

	Given Interval		Inverted Interval
Numerical Distance	Third	⟶	Sixth
Interval Name	Major	⟶	Minor

The numerical distance of an interval and its inversion always add up to nine. Therefore, the above third, when inverted, becomes a sixth.

$$(3 \text{ plus } \underline{} = 9)$$

The interval of a fourth, when inverted, becomes a fifth, and a second, when inverted, becomes a seventh, etc.

The interval name always changes when inverted, with the exception of a perfect interval.

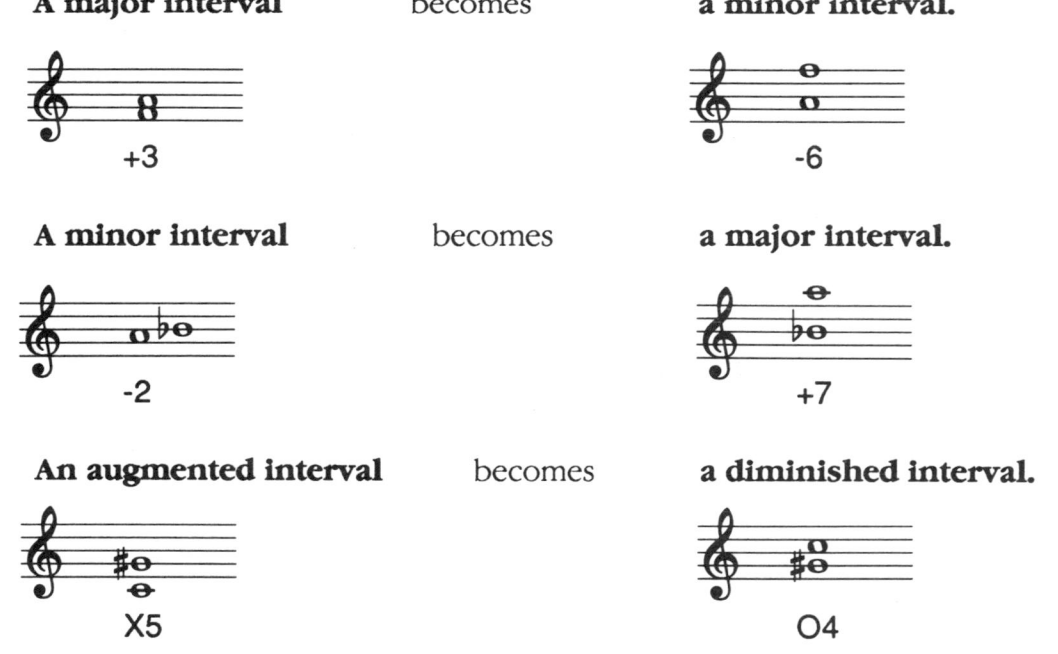

A major interval	becomes	**a minor interval.**
+3		-6
A minor interval	becomes	**a major interval.**
-2		+7
An augmented interval	becomes	**a diminished interval.**
X5		O4

A diminished interval   becomes   **an augmented interval.**

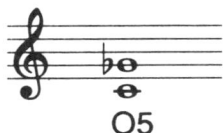

O5

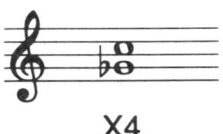

X4

Exception:

A perfect interval   *remains*   **a perfect interval.**

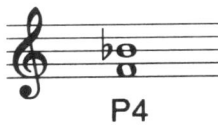

P4

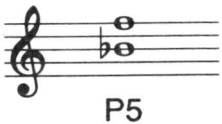

P5

Written Exercise

For each of the following:

a) Name the interval (1 mark).

b) Invert the lower note an octave higher and re-write the interval on the staff below (1 mark).

c) Re-name the interval (1 mark).

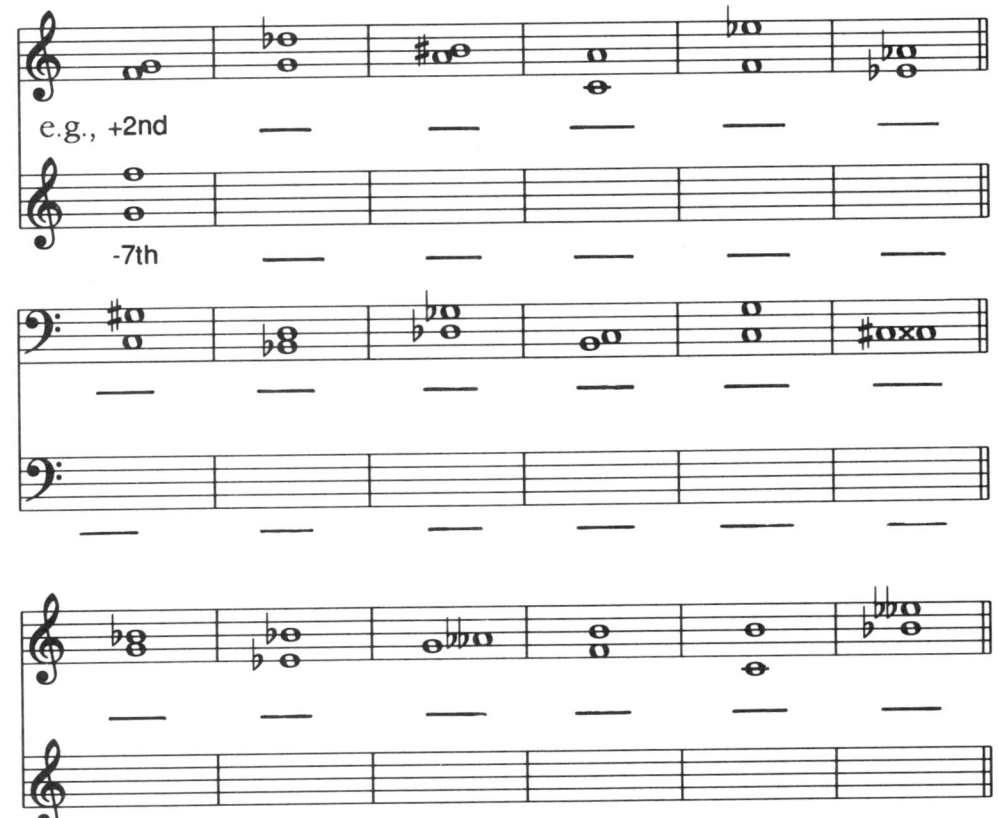

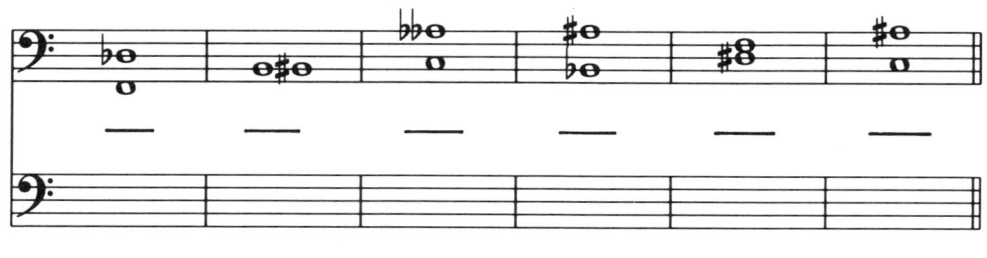

Perfect Score: 69   Student's Score:

Keyboard Exercise (optional)

a) Play and name aloud each of the following intervals.

b) Play each inverted interval and re-name aloud.

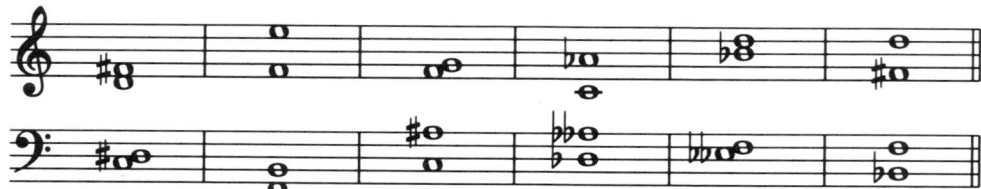

Review

1. An interval is the _____ or _____ in
    _____ between any two notes.

2. In all major scales, PERFECT intervals always occur on the _____
    _____ , _____ , and _____ degrees of the scale.

3. In all major scales, MAJOR intervals always occur on the _____
    _____ , _____ , and _____ degrees of the scale.

4. The _____ note of any interval is the keynote of the _____
    scale, and notes within the scale form either _____ or _____
    intervals from the _____ .

5. _____ intervals are written a _____ lower than MAJOR
    intervals and the _____ _____ is not found in the
    scale of the keynote.

6. When a PERFECT or MAJOR interval is made a _____ larger,
    it is called a _____ interval and the _____ _____
    is not found in the _____ scale of the keynote.

7. When a PERFECT or MINOR interval is made a _____ smaller,
    it is called a _____ interval and the _____ _____
    is not found in the _____ scale of the keynote.

8. To invert an interval, you write the _____ note an _____
    higher, or you write the _____ note an _____ lower.

9. When intervals are inverted, both the _____ _____ and the
    _____ name changes. An exception to this is the ____ interval.

10. The numerical distance of an interval and its _____ always add up
    to _____ .

11. The interval _____ always changes when inverted:
    a major interval becomes a _____ interval,
    a minor interval becomes a _____ interval,
    an augmented interval becomes a _____ interval,
    a diminished interval becomes an _____ interval.

Perfect Score: 49   **Student's Score:**

Chords

Major and Minor Triads

The **triad** is a special grouping of three notes called a **chord**. It consists of a **root** (the lowest note of the chord) and notes a **third** and **fifth** above it.

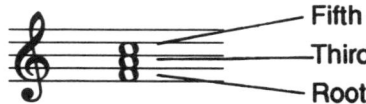

Triads may be written or played on any note of the major and harmonic minor scales. When writing the **dominant** triad of the **harmonic minor scale,** always remember that the third of the chord requires an accidental because this note is the leading note of the scale.

There are different kinds of triads, such as major and minor.

A **major** triad consists of a root and intervals of a **major** third and **perfect** fifth.

Here are tonic major triads built on the notes C and G.

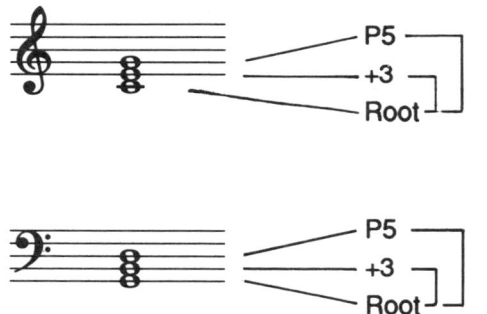

Write tonic major triads above the following keynotes:

Keyboard Exercise (optional)

Play the following tonic major triads, and listen in particular to the sound of the interval of the major third:

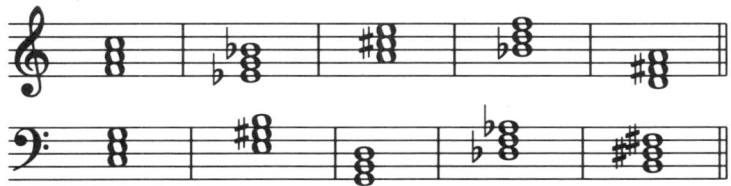

A **minor** triad consists of a root and intervals of a **minor** third and **perfect** fifth above it.

Here are tonic minor triads built on the notes C and G.

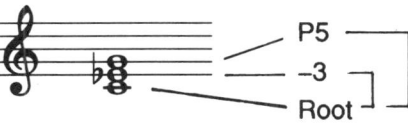

This is a tonic minor triad built on the note F sharp.

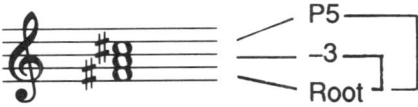

Write tonic minor triads above the following keynotes:

Keyboard Exercise (optional)

Play the following tonic minor triads, and listen in particular to the sound of the interval of the minor third.

Review Exercises

1. Indicate whether the following tonic triads are major or minor.

10 marks

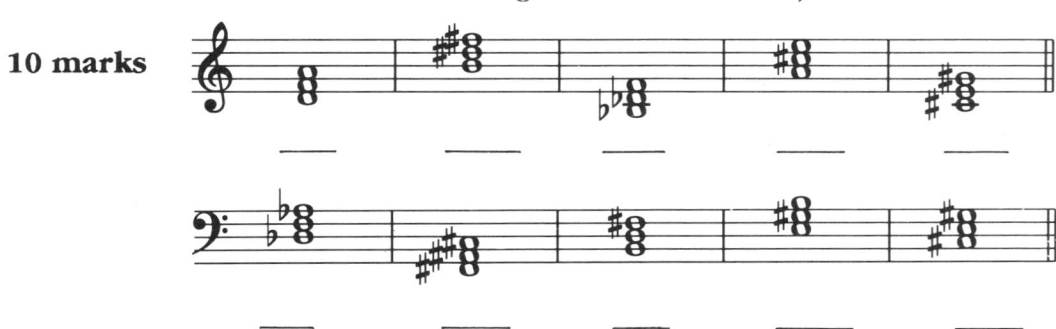

2. Write a tonic major triad above each of the given notes.

10 marks

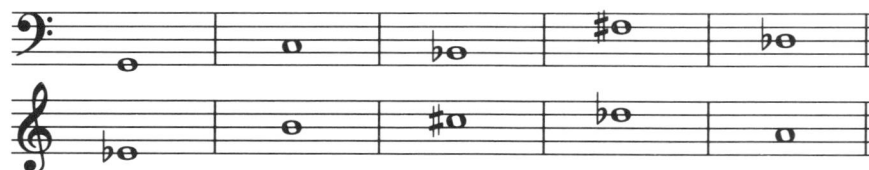

3. Write a tonic minor triad above each of the given notes.

10 marks

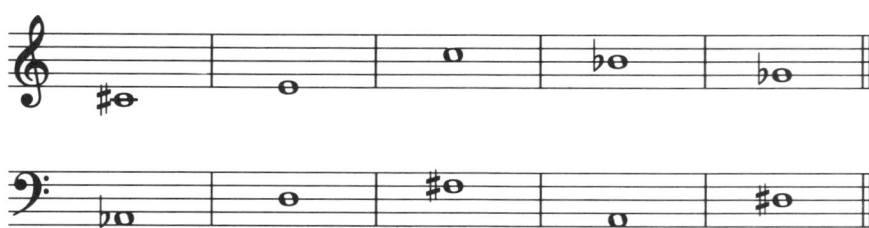

4. Change the following tonic major triads into tonic minor triads by lowering the third a chromatic semitone (1 mark), and name the key of the minor triad (1 mark).

16 marks

Key   F+   F-   _____   _____

5. Change the following tonic minor triads into tonic major triads by raising the third a chromatic semitone (1 mark), and name the key of the major triad (1 mark).

18 marks

Key

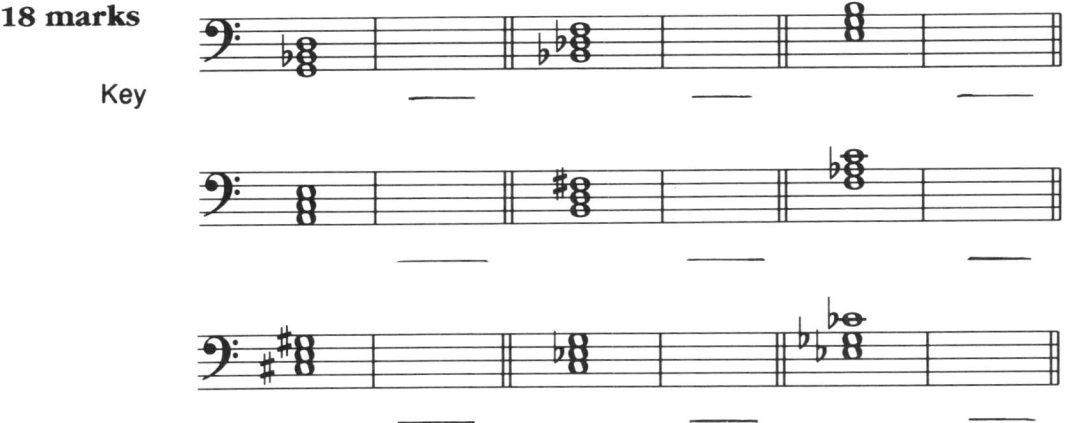

Keyboard Exercise (optional)

Play the following triads:

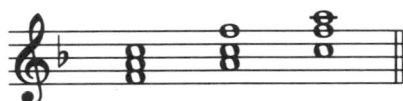

You have just played the root position, first inversion and second inversion of the tonic triad of F major.

A triad has two inversions.

Play the same triads once more, this time noticing how each time the bottom note is raised an octave to make the next inversion.

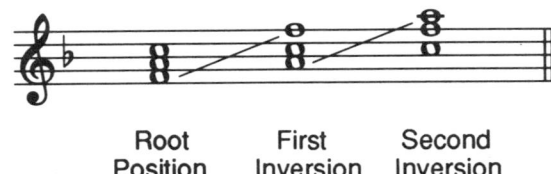

Root   First   Second
Position Inversion   Inversion

Inverted Triads

A triad whose notes are in the order of a root, third and fifth is in **root position.**

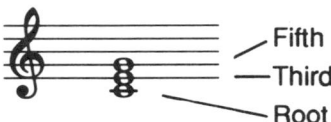

When the third of the triad is on the bottom, we say the triad is in the **first inversion.**

When the fifth of the triad is on the bottom, we say the triad is in the **second inversion.**

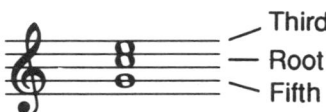

Written Exercise

Write the following root position triads in first and second inversions:

e.g.,

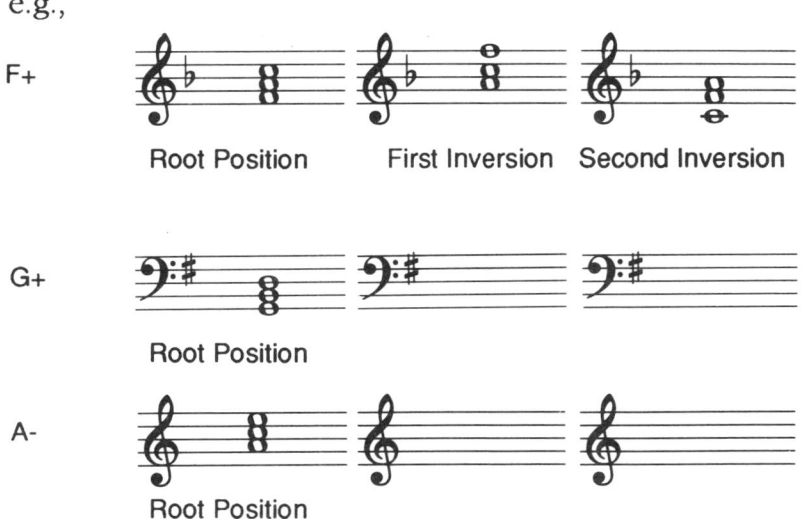

Keyboard Exercise (optional)

Play the following tonic triads and their inversions:

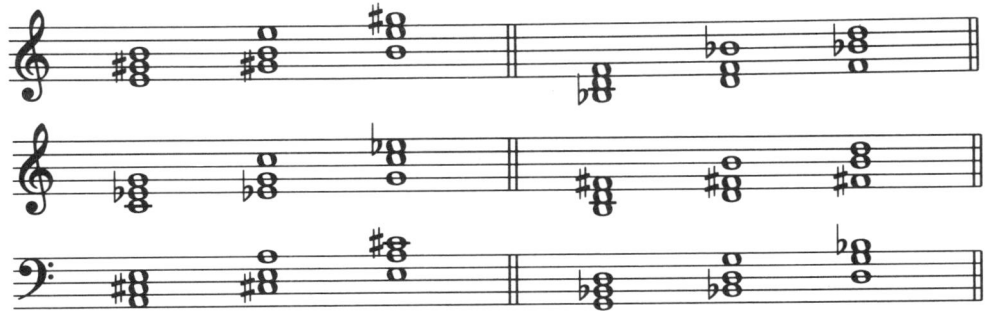

Identifying Major and Minor Triads

In order to identify given triads which are *not* in root position,

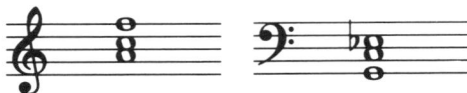

it is necessary to re-write the notes in the order of a root, third and fifth (root-position triad),

and the interval of the third determines whether the triad is major or minor.

Major Triad   Minor Triad

Review Exercises

1. Write the root position of each of the following tonic triads (1 mark), and add the necessary accidentals (1 mark).

Perfect Score: 20

Student's Score:

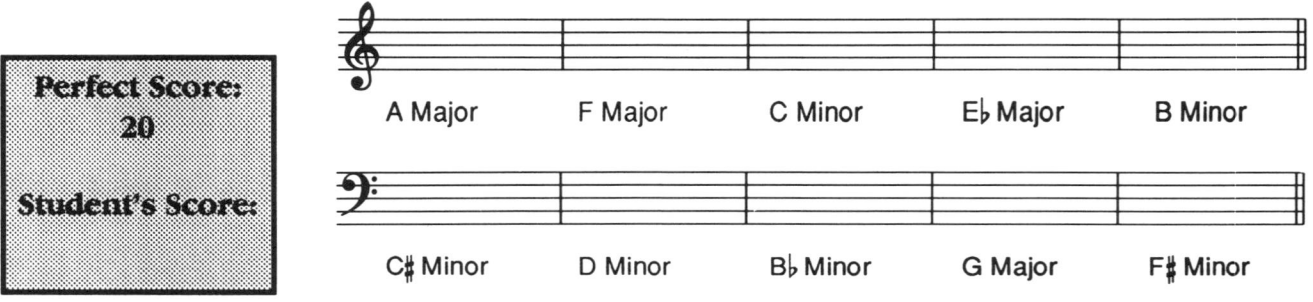

A Major   F Major   C Minor   E♭ Major   B Minor

C♯ Minor   D Minor   B♭ Minor   G Major   F♯ Minor

2. Write the first inversion of each of the following tonic triads (1 mark), and add the correct key signature (1 mark).

Perfect Score: 20

Student's Score:

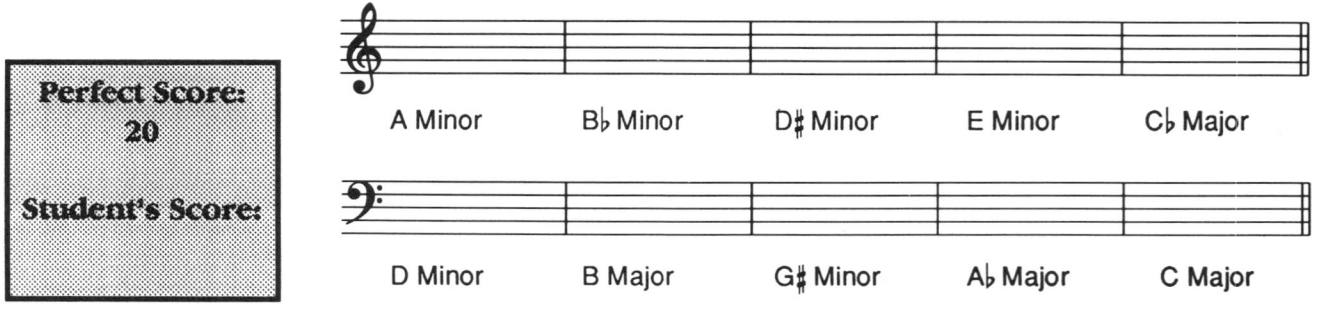

A Minor   B♭ Minor   D♯ Minor   E Minor   C♭ Major

D Minor   B Major   G♯ Minor   A♭ Major   C Major

3. Write the second inversion of each of the following tonic triads (1 mark), and add the necessary accidentals (1 mark).

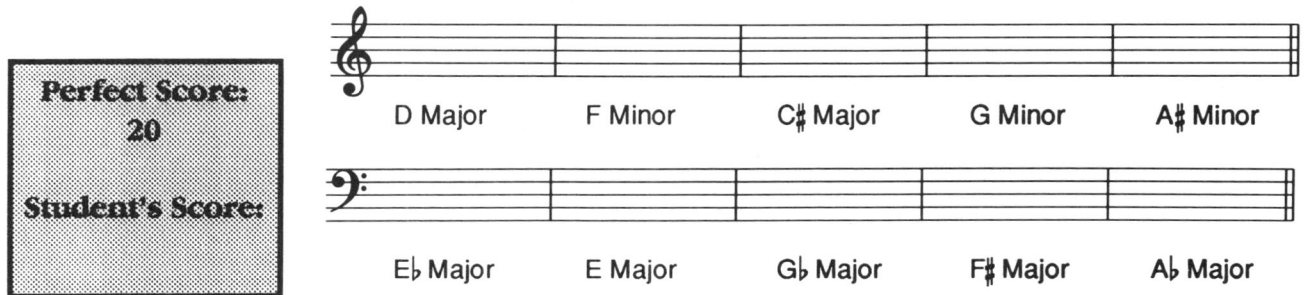

Perfect Score: 20

Student's Score:

| D Major | F Minor | C# Major | G Minor | A# Minor |

| Eb Major | E Major | Gb Major | F# Major | Ab Major |

4. Identify the following triads by naming the root and the kind of triad and position (root, first inversion or second inversion) (3 marks).

Root _____   _____   _____   _____   _____
Kind _____   _____   _____   _____   _____
Position _____   _____   _____   _____   _____

Root _____   _____   _____   _____   _____
Kind _____   _____   _____   _____   _____
Position _____   _____   _____   _____   _____

Root _____   _____   _____   _____   _____
Kind _____   _____   _____   _____   _____
Position _____   _____   _____   _____   _____

Perfect Score: 45   Student's Score:

5. Write the inversions of each of the following triads (2 marks):

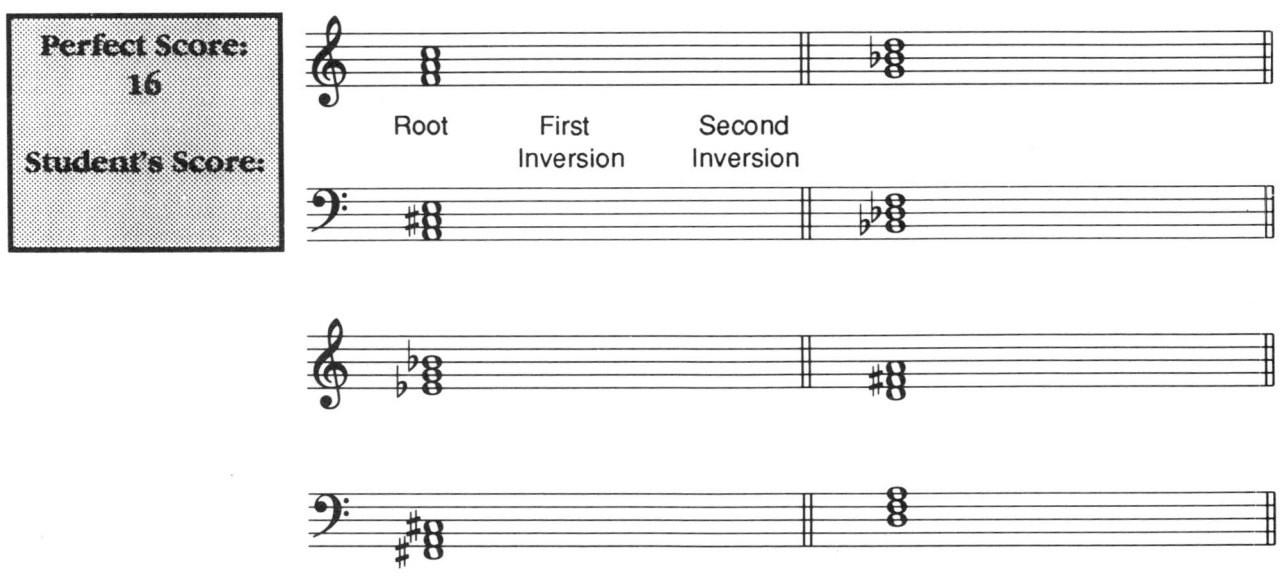

Perfect Score:
16

Student's Score:

6. Add accidentals to form the indicated tonic triads (1 mark).

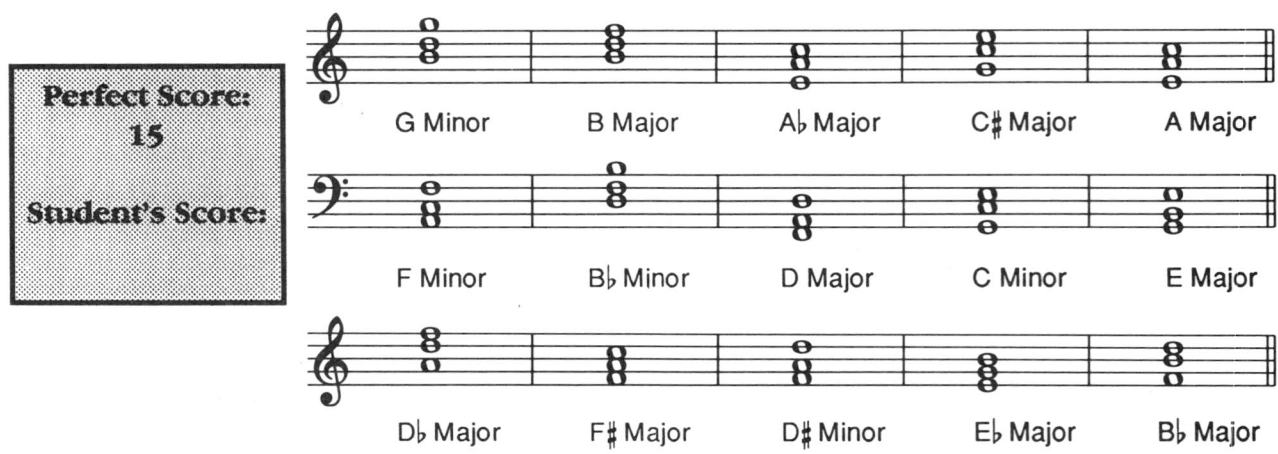

Perfect Score:
15

Student's Score:

7. Write the following triads in the treble clef on the staff provided (1 mark):

a) a major triad with A as the third

b) a minor triad with G as the fifth

c) a major triad with E flat as the root

d) a minor triad with F sharp as the fifth

e) a major triad with G sharp as the third

f) a minor triad with B flat as the root

Perfect Score:
6

Student's Score:

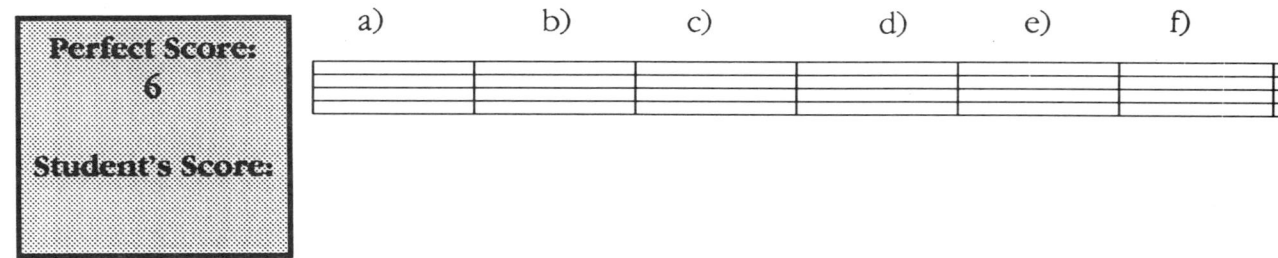

8. Remembering that triads may be written on any note of the major and harmonic minor scales, write the following triads in the bass clef using the correct key signature (2 marks):

Perfect Score: 14

Student's Score:

a) the root position of the mediant triad of A major

b) the first inversion of the leading note triad of G minor

c) the second inversion of the dominant triad of B flat minor

d) the root position of the tonic triad of F sharp major

e) the first inversion of the submediant triad of D flat major

f) the second inversion of the subdominant triad of C minor

g) the first inversion of the supertonic triad of F minor

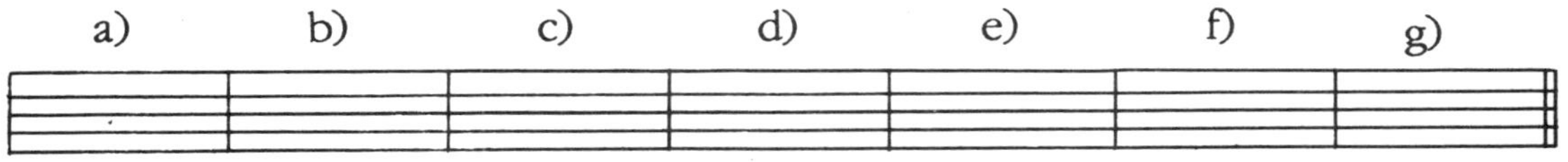

a)	b)	c)	d)	e)	f)	g)

Review

1. The triad is a____-note chord consisting of a_____and notes a_____ and a_____above it.

2. Triads may be written or played on any note of the_____and _____ _____scales.

3. When writing the_____triad of the_____minor scale, remember that the_____of the chord requires an_____, because this is the_____ _____of the scale.

4. There are different kinds of triads, such as_____and_____.

5. A major triad consists of a_____and intervals of a_____ _____ and a_____ _____.

6. A minor triad consists of a_____and intervals of a_____ _____ and a_____ _____.

7. A triad has_____inversions.

8. A triad whose notes are in the order of a_____, _____, and_____ is in root_____.

9. When the_____of the triad is on the bottom, we say the triad is in the _____ _____.

10. When the_____of the triad is on the bottom, we say the triad is in the _____ _____.

11. In order to identify major or minor triads which are not in the root position, it is necessary to re-write the notes in the order of a_____, _____, and_____. Then the interval of the_____determines whether the triad is major or minor.

Perfect Score: 40   Student's Score:

Naming the Keys of Melodies without Key Signatures

Finding the Major Key of a Melody

1. Collect the accidentals.

2. Put them in their correct key-signature order.

3. State the key.

To find the key of the above song:

1. The accidentals are C sharp and F sharp.

2. Their correct order is F sharp and C sharp.

3. Therefore, the key of the above melody is D major, as the key signature of D major is two sharps — F sharp and C sharp.

Remember —

If all the accidental sharps in a given melody can be written in the correct key-signature order, then the melody is in a major key. Similarly, when all the accidental flats in a given melody can be written in the correct key-signature order, then the melody is written in a major key.

Here is the same song re-written at the same pitch with its correct key signature.

Key of D major

Written Exercise

Name the keys of the following melodies, and re-write each melody at the same pitch with the correct key signature, omitting unnecessary accidentals (4 marks per question).

1.

List accidentals _____

Re-write in correct key signature order _____

Name the key _____

Re-write the melody with key signature:

2.

List accidentals _____

Re-write in correct key signature order _____

Name the key _____

Re-write the melody with key signature:

3.

List accidentals _____

Re-write in correct key signature order _____

Name the key _____

Re-write the melody with key signature:

4.

List accidentals _____

Re-write in correct key signature order _____

Name the key _____

Re-write the melody with key signature:

Perfect Score: 16   Student's Score:

Finding the Minor Key of a Melody

If all the accidentals in a given melody cannot be written in the correct key-signature order, then the melody is in a minor key.

To find the key of the above melody:

1. Collect the accidentals (B♮, E♭, A♭).

2. Write the accidentals as they would appear in the correct key-signature order (B♮, E♭, A♭).

3. The note in question is the missing B flat. It has been raised to B natural, as it is the leading note.

4. Therefore, the key of the above melody is C minor, as the key signature of C minor is three flats — B♭, E♭, A♭, with B♮ as the raised leading note.

Here is the melody re-written at the same pitch with the correct key signature.

Key of C minor

raised 7th (leading note)

Remember —

If all the accidental flats in a given melody cannot be written in the correct key-signature order, then the melody is in a minor key.

If all the accidental sharps in a given melody cannot be written in the correct key-signature order, then the melody is in a minor key.

Written Exercise

Re-write each of the following passages using the correct key signature, omitting the unnecessary accidentals (5 marks).

J. S. Bach

1.

List accidentals _____

Can they be written in their correct key-signature order? _____

The raised seventh is _____

The key is _____

Re-write the melody with key signature:

J. S. Bach

2.

List accidentals _____

Can they be written in their correct key-signature order? _____

The raised seventh is _____

The key is _____

Re-write the melody with key signature:

A. Corelli

3.

List accidentals _____

Can they be written in their correct key-signature order? _____

The raised seventh is _____

The key is _____

Re-write the melody with key signature:

J. S. Bach

4.

List accidentals _____

Can they be written in their correct key-signature order? _____

The raised seventh is _____

The key is _____

Re-write the melody with key signature:

5.

List accidentals _____

Can they be written in their correct key-signature order? _____

The raised seventh is _____

The key is _____

Re-write the melody with key signature:

6.

List accidentals _____

Can they be written in their correct key-signature order? _____

The raised seventh is _____

The key is _____

Re-write the melody with key signature:

Perfect Score: 30   Student's Score:

Review

1. To name the key of a melody without a key signature, you must

   a) collect the_____,

   b) put them in their correct_____,

   c) state the_____of the melody.

2. If all the_____sharps in a melody can be written in their correct
   _____-_____, then the melody is in a_____key.

3. If all the_____flats in a melody can be written in their correct
   _____-_____, then the melody is in a_____key.

4. If all the_____flats in a melody cannot be written in their correct
   _____-_____, then the melody is in a_____key.

5. If all the_____sharps in a melody cannot be written in their correct
   _____-_____, then the melody is in a_____key.

6. When the accidentals in a given melody cannot be written in the correct
   key-signature order, the note in question is the_____ _____
   or_____note which must be retained in the music.

Perfect Score: 22   Student's Score:

Transposition

In Book One we learned how to transpose melodies up or down an octave from one clef to another.

Transposition may also involve playing or writing a melody in a key other than the original one.

At this level we will deal with transposition only from one major key to another major key.

In transposing a melody you must know the key of the original or given melody. Sometimes the key signature is given as shown.

Key: A♭ Major

If the key signature is *not* given, you must collect the accidentals to determine the major key.

Key: A Major (F♯, C♯, G♯)

Sometimes the name of the new key is given, and one just transposes the music up the required interval from the original key to the new key. Example: Transpose the following melody into the key of B major:

Original Key: A major

Transposed into B major

The key signature of the new key (B major) has been inserted and each note of the original melody in A major has been written the interval of a second higher.

Sometimes the name of the new key is not given, and you are asked to transpose the music up a required interval.

Example:

Transpose the following melody up a major third (meaning a major third interval higher than the tonic of the original key).

Original Key: C major

A major third up from the original key (C major) is E.

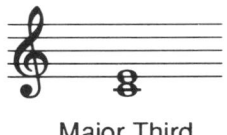

Major Third

The key signature of the new key (E major) is inserted and each note of the original melody raised a third.

Transposed up a major third to E major

If the passage to be transposed has accidentals, then the transposition itself will have accidentals occurring next to the same notes.

Accidentals may or may not be of the same kind and care must be taken to consider exactly what effect (raised or lowered notes) the accidentals have in the original key and treat them the same in the new key.

Example: Transpose the following melody up a minor third.

Original Key: A major

Transposed into new key: C major

How are the accidentals treated so that the effect in the new key is the same as in the original?

Written Exercises

1. Transpose each of the following passages up a major third (2 marks).

a)

b)

c)

d)

1. Transpose each of the following passages up a minor third (2 marks).

a)

b)

3. Transpose each of the following passages up a perfect fourth (2 marks).

a)

b)

c)

Perfect Score: 6   Student's Score:

4. Transpose each of the following passages up a major second (2 marks).

a)

b)

Perfect Score: 4   Student's Score:

5.

a) Transpose this passage into the key of B major (2 marks).

b) Transpose this passage into the key of G major (2 marks).

c) Transpose this passage into the key of E flat major (2 marks).

d) Transpose this passage into the key of E major (2 marks).

e) Transpose this passage into the key of C major (2 marks).

f) Transpose this passage into the key of A flat major (2 marks).

Perfect Score: 12   Student's Score:

Keyboard Exercises (optional)

At the keyboard, transpose each of the following folk songs as indicated:

1. "Frere Jacques"
    a) into G major
    b) into A major

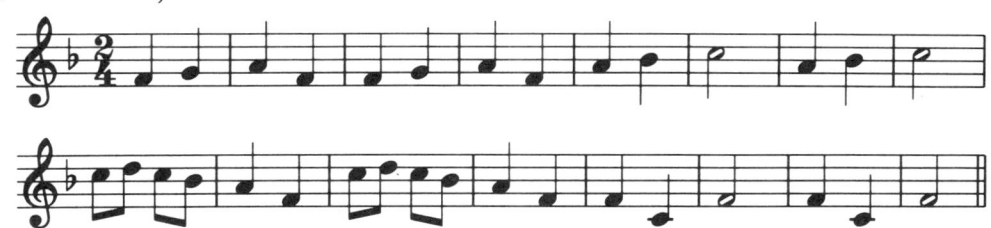

2. "C'est L'Aviron"
    a) into F major
    b) into E flat major

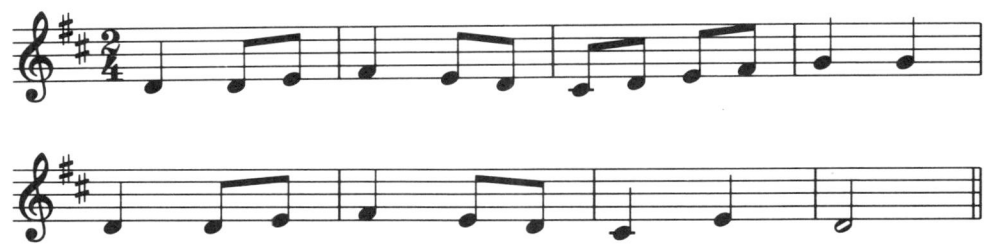

3. "D'ou Viens-Tu Bergere"
    a) into A major
    b) into C major

4. "Un Canadien Errant"
   a) up a major second
   b) up a major third

Cadences

Every piece of music is divided and subdivided into phrases. Each phrase has a two-chord ending called a **cadence.**

The Perfect Cadence

Keyboard Exercises (optional)

Play the following passage twice, each time listening closely to the sound of the cadence.

The above cadence is called a **perfect cadence.**

Have you noticed how final sounding it is? The perfect cadence consists of the dominant chord (V) followed by the tonic chord (I).

Play the following examples of perfect cadences:

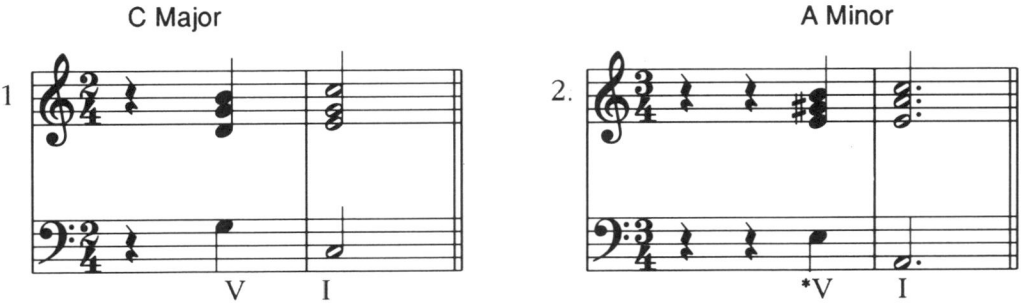

*Remember that the leading note requires an accidental in the minor key. Notice how the final chord of each cadence is usually on the strong beat.

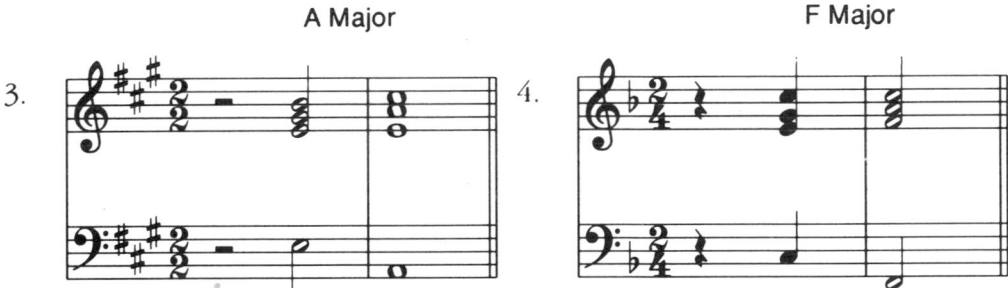

Writing Cadences

In the above examples note the following:

a) The root of each chord is written in the bass voice.

b) All three notes of the dominant chord (G, B, D) are written in the treble clef in any order.

c) All three notes of the tonic chord (C, E, G) are written in the treble clef in any order.

d) The note which is the same (common) between the two triads is generally kept in the same part. In C major the common note is G, as indicated above (↔)

e) The other two treble notes of the dominant chord (in this case B and D) move up a second.

Written Exercises

Using the previous examples as a guide, write two-bar examples of perfect cadences in the given time signature (2 marks). Insert the correct key signature (1 mark).

Perfect Score: 30   Student's Score:

Keyboard Exercise (optional)

At the keyboard, transpose each of the above perfect cadences written in major keys up a major second.

The Plagal Cadence
Keyboard Exercise (optional)

Play the following passage twice, each time listening closely to the sound of the cadence.

IV   I

Subdominant Tonic
Chord   Chord

Plagal Cadence

The above cadence is called a **plagal cadence.** It is very final sounding, as well. It is sometimes referred to as an "Amen" cadence, because it is frequently used for the ending of hymns. The plagal cadence consists of the subdominant chord (IV) followed by the tonic chord (I).

Play the following examples of plagal cadences:

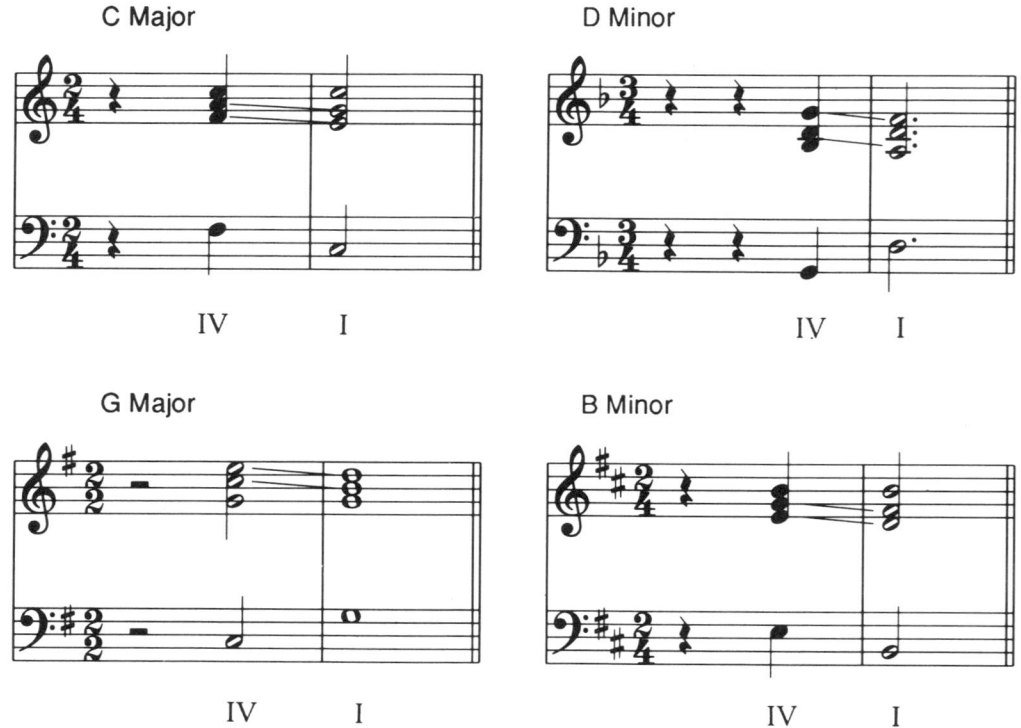

Plagal cadences are written in the same manner as perfect cadences (see page 92). There is one exception — two treble notes of the subdominant chord move down a second, as shown in the above examples.

Written Exercises

Using the previous examples as a guide, write two-bar examples of plagal cadences in the time signature and key indicated (2 marks).

C Major   B Flat Major

Perfect Score: 20   Student's Score:

Keyboard Exercise (optional)

At the keyboard, transpose each of the above plagal cadences written in major keys up a major second.

Review

1. Transposition may involve transposing melodies up or down an octave from one_____to another, or the playing or writing of melodies in keys other than the_____.

2. In transposing a melody, you must know what_____the original melody is in.

3. If the key signature is not given, you must collect the_____ to determine the key.

4. Sometimes the name of the new key is given and on just transposes the music up the required_____from the_____key to the_____ key.

5. Sometimes the name of the new key is not given, and you are asked to _____the music up a required_____.

6. If the passage to be transposed has accidentals, then the transposition will have_____occurring next to the_____notes.

7. Accidentals may or may not be the_____kind, and care must be taken to consider exactly what_____the accidentals have in the _____key and treat them the same in the_____key.

8. Every piece of music is divided and subdivided into_____.

9. Each phrase has a_____-_____ _____called a_____.

10. A perfect cadence consists of the_____ _____followed by the _____ _____.

11. The leading note always repuires an_____in the minor key.

12. The plagal cadence consists of the_____ _____ followed by the_____ _____.

Perfect Score: 29   Student's Score:

Correction of Errors

Written Exercise

How many errors are you able to find in the following passages? Re-write each passage correctly on the staff provided.

9 marks

1.

6 marks

Ala marcia

2.

5 marks

3.

10 marks

4.

9 marks

5.

Perfect Score: 39   Student's Score: (Answers at back of book.)

Test Paper

Time Limit — Two Hours

a) *Read* each question carefully before answering.

b) Write clearly.

c) Upon completion of the test, re-read each question and answer several times.

d) Turn to page 104 and mark your own paper.

1. Write the following scales, using the correct key signature for each:

    a) A flat major (ascending only) in the bass clef
    b) B minor harmonic (ascending and descending) in the treble clef
    c) C sharp minor melodic (ascending and descending) in the bass clef

a)

b)

c)

2. Write the following intervals above the note E:

    a) a major third
    b) a perfect fourth
    c) an augmented second
    d) a diminished seventh
    e) a minor sixth

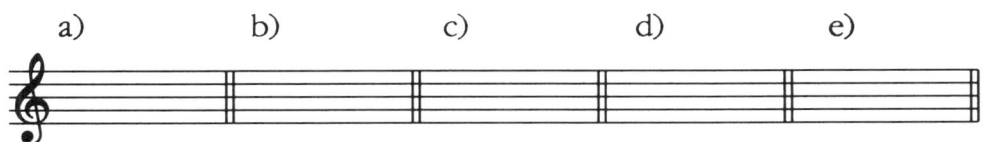

3. Invert the intervals in Question 2 and re-name them.

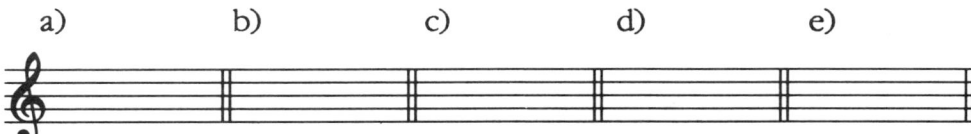

4. Write the following notes in the bass clef, using the correct key signature for each:

a) the supertonic of E major
b) the leading note of G minor
c) the dominant of B flat major
d) the mediant of F minor

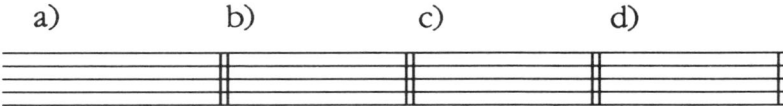

5. Copy the passage below at the same pitch. Insert the correct key signature and omit the unnecessary accidentals. Name the key.

Key _____

6. Write the following triads in the treble clef, using accidentals instead of a key signature:

    a) the root position of the tonic triad of A flat major
    b) the first inversion of the dominant triad of E minor
    c) the second inversion of the tonic triad of F major

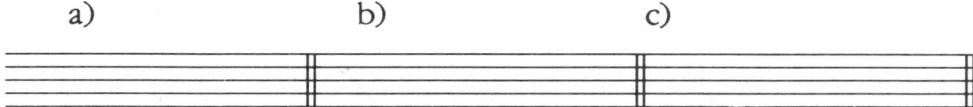

7. Transpose the following passage a major third higher.

8. Complete each of the following bars by adding rests as indicated:

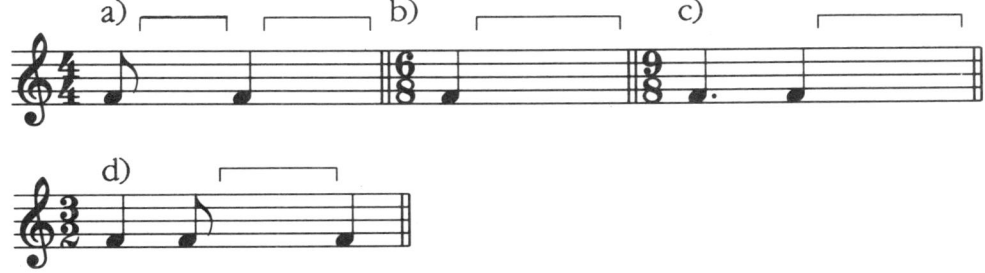

9. Write a two-bar example of each of the following cadences. Use a ¾ time signature and insert the correct key signatures.

    a) a perfect cadence in G major
    b) a perfect cadence in F minor
    c) a plagal cadence in B flat major

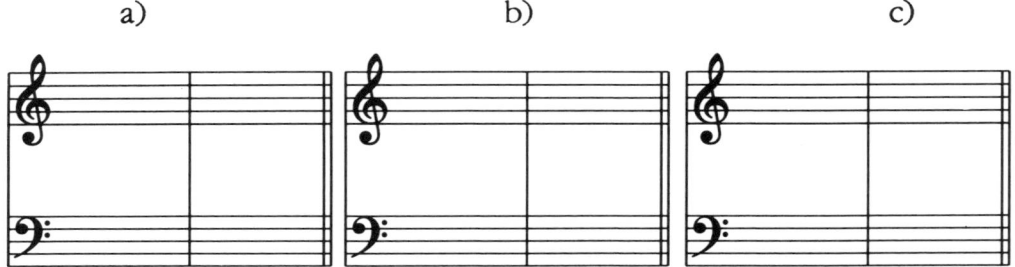

10. Correct the errors in the following passage:

11. Explain the following terms:

    a) *moderato* _____

    b) *vivace* _____

    c) *una corda* _____

    d) *cantabile* _____

Answers to the Theory Test

Marks

15   1.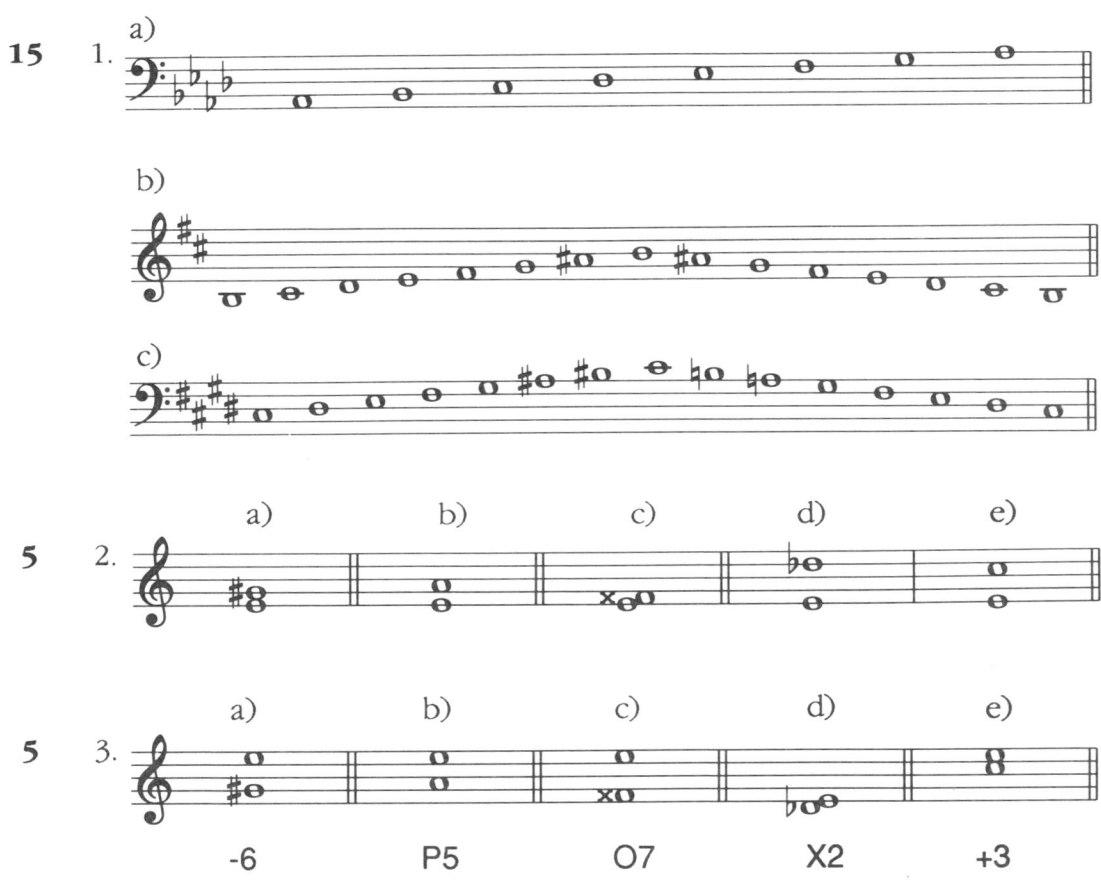

5   2.

5   3.

          -6   P5   O7   X2   +3

8   4.

10   5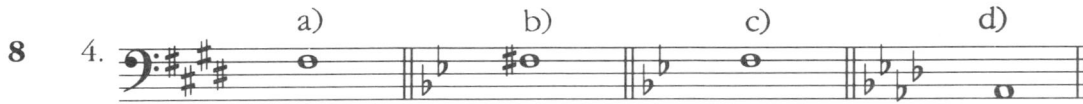

Key — D Major

10 6.

8 7.

10 8.

12 9.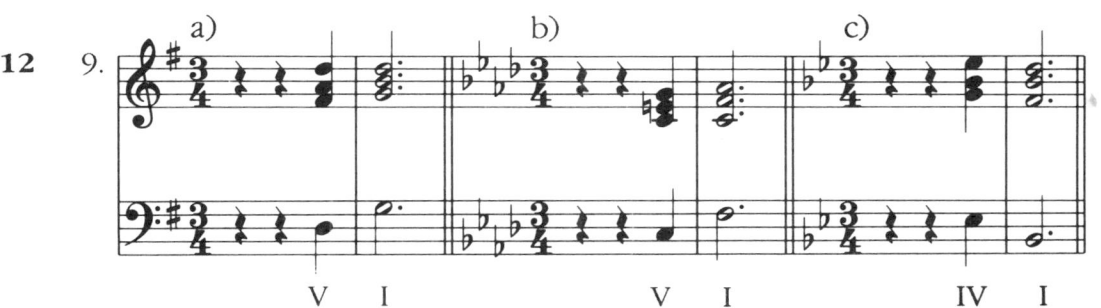

V   I   V   I   IV   I

9 10.

8 11. *moderato* — in moderate time
vivace — lively
una corda — depress the soft pedal
cantabile — in a singing style

Common Terms and Signs

It is the author's belief that this area of study should be related directly to practical work. A knowledge of terms, signs and composers forms an important part of the study of every musical composition. This knowledge enables the student to achieve a better overall understanding of the music.

The piano piece on this page might serve as a guide to reviewing some of the terms and signs. (The student should similarly play and observe the markings in the pieces reviewed in the graded books.)

Sarah's Lullaby

J. Lawless

Terms and Signs

Andante — At a moderate speed, flowing.

Dolce — Sweetly.

p — Softly.

pp — Very softly.

ppp — As softly as possible.

3/4 — Time signature.

⌒ — A slur — play smoothly and singing.

⌐___¬ — A pedal.

◁ — Crescendo.

▷ — Diminuendo.

♩__♩ — A tie.

Rit. — Gradually getting slower.

Students trying the Grade One Theory examination of the Royal Conservatory of Music of Toronto are required to know the meanings of the following terms and signs.

Accelerando — Gradually getting quicker.

Accent — 𝅘𝅥 — Special emphasis on a note.

Adagio — Very slowly.

A tempo — In time, a return to the original speed.

Alla — In the style of.

Allegretto — Fairly quickly.

Allegro — Lively, quick, bright.

Andante — At a moderate speed, flowing.

Andantino — Generally meaning a little faster than andante.

Animoso — Lively, spirited.

Assai — Very.

Ben — Well, much.

Brillante — Brilliant.

Cantabile — In a singing style.

Col. colla — With the.

Coll 8ᵛᵃ — To play the same notes in octaves.

Con — With

Con brio — With brightness, with spirit.

Con espressione — With expression.

Con moto — With motion, with spirit.

Crescendo — ⊂ — Gradually louder.

Da capo, D.C. — Repeat from the beginning.

Dal segno, D.S. — Repeat from the sign 𝄋

Decrescendo — ⊃ — Gradually softer

Diminuendo — ⊃ — Gradually softer.

Dolce — Sweetly.

E, ed — And.

Espressivo — Expressively.

Fine — The end.

Forte — ***f*** — Loudly.

Forte piano — ***fp*** — Loudly, then softly immediately.

Fortissimo — ***ff*** — Very loudly.

Grave — Slowly, solemnly.

Grazioso — Gracefully.

Larghetto — A little faster than largo.

Largo — Very slowly, slower than adagio.

Legato — Smoothly.

Leggiero — Lightly.

Lento — Slow.

Loco — To play at the written pitch after 8va.

Ma — But.

Maestoso — Majestically.

Marcato — Well marked.

M.D. — (Mano destra) — With the right hand.

M.S. — (Mano sinistra) — With the left hand.

Meno — Less.

Meno mosso — Less movement.

M.M. — (Maelzels metronomes). This sign, with a note and number following indicates the number of beats played per minute, e.g., M.M. ♩ = 80 (eighty quarter notes per minute).

Mezzo forte — **mf** — A little softer than forte.

Mezzo piano — **mp** — A little louder than piano.

Moderato — At a moderate speed.

Molto — Very much.

Non — Not.

Non troppo — Not too much.

Ottava, 8va — When placed above notes, this means the notes are to be played an octave higher. When placed below notes, this means the notes are to be played an octave lower.

Pause — ⌢ — Written over a note or rests, this sign means to hold the note or rest longer than its normal value.

Pianissimo — **pp** — Very softly.

Piano — **p** — Softly.

Più — More.

Più mosso — More movement.

Poco — Little.

Poco a poco — Little by little.

Prestissimo — As fast as possible.

Presto — Very fast.

Quasi — Like.

Rallentando — Gradually getting slower.

Repeat signs — The measures within the repeat signs are to be played twice.

Ritardando — Gradually getting slower.

Sempre — Always.

Senza — Without.

Slur — — A line drawn over two or more notes of different pitch to show they are to be played legato.

Staccato — — a note that is to be played short or detached.

Tempo — Time.

Tempo primo — In the original time.

Tempo rubato — In robbed time.

Tenuto — To hold, sustain.

Tie — — A curved line joining two notes of the same pitch, though not necessarily of the same time value, used to lengthen the time value of a note.

Tranquillo — Quiet.

Troppo — Too much.

Vivace — Lively, spirited.

Answers to Written Exercises

(page 98)

1.

2.
Alla marcia

3.

4.

5.

Appendix

accidentals 8
cadences 91
cadences, perfect 91
cadences, plagal 94
cadences, writing 92
chords 64
compound time, grouping notes in 38
compound time, grouping rests in 39
compound time, a special word about 34
errors, correction of 98
flats, double 10
intervals 54
intervals, augmented 55
intervals, diminished 55
intervals, inversion of 59
intervals, major 54
intervals, minor 54
intervals, perfect 54
key signatures, grouping of sharps and flats in 14
key signatures, naming the keys of melodies without 75
melody, finding the major key of a 75
melody, finding the minor key of a 78
note groups, irregular 43
scales, degrees of 5
scales, harmonic minor — order of tones and semitones 25
scales, major 11
scales, major — order of tones and semitones 11
scales, major — naming intervals of notes in 54
scales, major naming intervals of notes not in 54
scales, melodic minor — order of tones and semitones 27
scales, minor 25
scales, technical names 5
syncopation 41
syncopation, natural 42
syncopation, usual 42
terms and signs, common 106
time, compound 34
time signatures, irregular 41
transposition 82
triads, identifying major and minor 70
triads, inverted 68
triads, major and minor 64